creative ESSENTIALS

STEPHEN FOLLOWS

HOW TO CROWDFUND YOUR FILM

creative ESSENTIALS

First published in 2018 by Kamera Books
an imprint of Oldcastle Books,
PO Box 394, Harpenden, Herts, AL5 1XJ
www.kamerabooks.com

ISBN
978-0-85730-183-3 (print)
978-0-85730-184-0 (epub)

2 4 6 8 10 9 7 5 3 1

Typeset by Elsa Mathern in Franklin Gothic 9.5 pt
Printed and bound by CPI Group (UK) Ltd, Croydon, CR0 4YY

CONTENTS

INTERVIEWS

FOREWORD

In 1885 the US found itself in the embarrassing position of being given a lovely statue by France, with nothing to put it on. So the American Committee of the Statue of Liberty established a crowdfunding campaign to raise the $100,000 needed to build the all-important plinth. After it was featured on the cover of Joseph Pulitzer's *New York World* newspaper, they finally really did it, raising $101,091 ($2.4 million in today's money) from over 160,000 donors.

Although crowdfunding has changed since 1885, there are lessons to be learnt from this story...

- First, that if you have a passion project which lacks a business case it is still possible to raise the money you need

- Second, that getting press coverage is essential to raising large amounts of money

- Finally, don't accept a gift until you know where you're going to put it

In the modern era, crowdfunding is considerably easier, with a whole host of sites and services offering to help you raise the money you need. (That said, if Kickstarter had been around for the Statue of Liberty campaign, I have no doubt the top reward would have been to have your face used as the model for Lady Liberty.)

The money you raise via crowdfunding is the best form of film financing possible...

- You don't have to pay it back

- You don't have any interest to pay

- No one controls your film

- You keep 100% of the film's profits

- You'll have started to build a loyal following way before the film has even been made

- It's open to everyone

The vast majority of crowdfunding sites don't charge up front fees, preferring instead to charge a percentage of the money you raise (typically around 5%). While projects trying to raise a lot may need to spend money creating a slick campaign, these costs are optional and you can usually substitute financial costs for time and effort. So, all you really need is an internet connection and the drive to work incredibly hard.

And that's at the heart of how crowdfunding works – you convert your time, effort and passion into money. The more you put in, the more you'll get out. There is a common misconception that in order to raise film finance via crowdfunding you need to already have a bunch of rich friends and family members. While there's no doubt this helps, it's not the main reason why successful campaigns work.

Very few of us have a large (or rich) enough base of loved ones to fund our next project, let alone the one after that. However, we're storytelling experts who seek to delight and entertain strangers via compelling narratives. We have chosen a life of crafting stories that make people laugh, cry, jump and think. And that's catnip to the kinds of people who back crowdfunding campaigns.

Pity the poor technologist who has invented a new type of drone that talks to your coffee-maker to ensure you have coffee waiting for you when you get home. Sure, they have an awesome product (I'd buy one) but they have to learn from scratch how to connect emotionally with strangers in order to raise their funds.

We filmmakers, on the other hand, have been practising for years – we write in cafes, shoot at dawn and cut in the dark. We can save the cat, hit the mark, check the gate, over-crank, flash-forward, flash-back, jump cut and all without ever crossing the line (although some things will be fixed in post).

We make people pay attention and give a damn and you're telling me there's a way of using that to raise money I never have to pay back? Yippie Ki Yay, master filmmakers.

So how do you do it?

Well, this is where this book can help. I have distilled data on almost 50,000 film crowd-funding campaigns as well as interviews with filmmakers, experts and employees of major crowdfunding platforms.

Together, they have helped me zero in on what makes filmmakers succeed (and the pitfalls to avoid) during the crowdfunding journey.

There's no doubt in my mind that online crowdfunding is one of the best things to happen to the world of independent film finance and so it's a real pleasure to help provide some guidance on how filmmakers can take full advantage of this revolution.

Go forth, fund and then film!

Stephen Follows
December 2017
You can read more of Stephen's research into the film industry at stephenfollows.com

INTRODUCTION TO **CROWDFUNDING**

Let's start by going through the basics. Then, later in the book, we'll get into the detailed nitty-gritty.

TRADITIONAL FUNDING SOURCES VS CROWDFUNDING

The best way to approach things is from the point of view of you, the filmmaker. You have a script, a plan and a team ready, so you're looking for finance.

One method would be to use some of the film industry's traditional funding models. But there are flaws in that plan.

First, you may not get the money. The people holding the purse strings can be quite cautious and tend to fund the types of films and film-makers that have succeeded before. It can be hard to break in.

If you can convince the powers that be to give you the money, that's fantastic, but they may

want things in return you're not willing to give up, for example:

- Ownership of the intellectual property, such as the idea, script and rights to the film

- Control over the process, such as how the film is made, when and where it's shot and who's in it

- Control over the artistic vision, including final cut

They're seeing it as a commercial product whereas you might be viewing it as a work of art or story you really want to tell. So, even if you can get access to funding via this method, it may not suit you.

Another option is to borrow the money from a bank or private investors. This can be quite hard because you'll need a business plan, sales projections and an established route to market. Even if you do convince someone to give you the money, in return they're going to want a guarantee that the investment will be coming back with

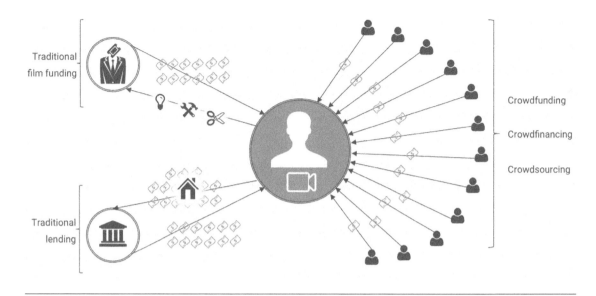

FIG 1.1 WHAT IS CROWDFUNDING? CROWDFUNDING METHODS SOURCE FUNDS FROM A WIDER POOL OF PEOPLE AND CAN AVOID THE CREATIVE OR FINANCIAL COMPROMISES THAT COME WITH FUNDS FROM PRODUCTION COMPANIES OR LARGER LENDERS

interest. This may involve you underwriting it by putting up any assets you have, such as your home. And no matter how well or badly the film performs, you still owe that money.

So, if you've decided against raising private finance or borrowing the money, or if the industry has decided against you and no one will lend to you, where can you turn?

This is where crowdfunding comes in. Crowdfunding is a method of fundraising where you ask a large number of people for small amounts of money.

This might be in a closed community where you're appealing to people you already know, like through a club or organisation, or maybe your friends and family. Or it could be online, where crowdfunding is most powerful because you can reach out to new people all over the world and tap into their existing networks to build up your own community.

Donations are typically quite small. Later on in the book we'll look at how much people give and why, but if you can build a large enough donor base the total amount you raise can be quite high. People have raised millions for feature films using crowdfunding.

CROWDFUNDING, CROWD FINANCING AND CROWD SOURCING

Crowdfunding is sometimes called **crowd financing**. In the film industry, when filmmakers say they're looking for funding, they tend to be focused on the film they want to make rather than the likely monetary return. It's not that they don't want to make money, simply that it's not their main focus. By contrast, business professionals and experts in the film industry who deal with money tend to talk about 'financing'.

The implicit suggestion when you use the word finance is that the people giving you the money have a financial stake in the success of the film.

So, crowd financing tends to be used when seeking commercial investors who will expect something significant in return, such as shares in your production company. Crowdfunding, on the other hand, tends to relate to no-strings donations. Contributors might be sent a T-shirt or mug or something like that (see **Rewards-based Crowdfunding**, below), but they don't own a stake in the film.

Crowd sourcing is when you go to the same pool of people, but instead of them chipping in money for equipment, food and locations, they give you the actual items. So you might say, 'Okay, everybody, here is my campaign. I need one camera, seven lights and a film crew.' People will then chip in with 'I'll give you a camera', 'I can give you some of the lights', 'I'll volunteer to be on the crew', etcetera.

CROWDFUNDING MODELS

The term crowdfunding actually covers four different models:

- **Rewards-based.** This is one you're probably familiar with. The donors give money in return for predefined rewards, sometimes called 'perks'. That might be a T-shirt or mug or whatever, but these are defined in advance. This money is effectively a donation in return for the reward, so there's no investment. There's no share of the profits or any control over the process. The filmmaker stays in control and if the film makes any money it's totally up to the filmmaker what they do with

that. The two most famous sites, which we'll focus on a lot in this book, are Indiegogo and Kickstarter. They run campaigns slightly differently, as we'll see, but fundamentally they sit in the category of rewards-based crowdfunding.

- **Donations.** Sometimes people give money in return for nothing more than the warm glow inside, or to see the project actually happen. This is charitable giving. There are a number of crowdfunding websites that are designed to raise money for causes and charities. These rarely actually relate to film because, although your film may be art that's worth creating, being a fully registered charity is quite a leap, so we're not going to be focusing on this here.

- **Equity.** This is what people often mean when they say 'crowd financing'. When the investors give you money, they get a share of the company or the profits. So you may or may not have to repay the original amount, but you definitely have to give them whatever share of the profits was agreed, and it may involve their having some control over the film. A couple of the sites that do this are Slated, which we're going to go through in detail later on, and also Crowdfunder.

- **Peer-to-peer lending.** This is where you borrow little bits of money from a large number of people. Rather than there being one bank that can say yes or no, it's lots of individuals with little bits of money to spare, who want to make a profit back. The advantage of this over a normal bank is that you probably don't have to put up as much collateral. And there isn't one person who is the key decision-

	Rewards based	Donation	Equity	Peer-to-peer lending	Hybrid models
Summary	Money given in return for pre-defined rewards	Charitable giving without tangible outcome	Selling shares in the company and / or profits	Lending by individuals, rather than banks etc.	Hybrid platforms combine two or more models
Main aim of donors	Rewards such as access or products	Support the cause or organisation	Profit	Interest	Depends on model
Free from repayment?	✓	✓	?	✗	?
You keep 100% of profits?	✓	✓	✗	✓	?
Keep complete creative control?	✓	✓	?	✓	?
Examples	INDIEGOGO KICKSTARTER	gofundme causes	slated Crowdfunder.co.uk	zopa Funding Circle	FUNDABLE FundedByMe

FIG 1.2 CROWDFUNDING MODELS

maker; instead, it's a whole group of people who are using these websites, like Funding Circle, where they get to choose how they're going to invest their money.

It's also possible to have a hybrid of some of these and there are platforms which mix and match elements from each.

When you're deciding which method you want to use for your film, you need to think about how much you're raising, what you're willing to give up and what you're not, and what has successfully been done by other companies in the past.

One of the things to consider is what will happen if you raise more than you were originally hoping for. Say you're trying to raise $100,000 and you end up raising $110,000. For rewards-based or donations it's not a problem, so long as you have enough rewards to send people in return.

But for equity or peer-to-peer lending there may be an issue with taking more money. With equity you're going to be giving up some of your company; once you sell 51% you could lose control of the company, and once 100% of the shares are gone you can't sell any more. With peer-to-peer lending you have to be aware that you're paying interest and so the more money you borrow, the more you have to pay back.

REWARDS-BASED CROWDFUNDING

Let's look at rewards-based crowdfunding in a bit more detail. We start with you, the filmmaker. You know the film you want to make, you've done your budget, you've got your team together, and now you just need the funds. Let's say you use a website like Indiegogo or Kickstarter to put together a crowdfunding campaign.

You use images, a main campaign video and text detailing what you're trying to do on a single campaign page. On that page you'll set up a number of rewards. For example, you might say those who donate £10 or above will be given access to a download of one of your previous films. For £20, maybe you'll send out a copy of the DVD of the new film when it's finished. The best rewards are interesting or unusual, so if your film is about astronauts, for example, you might want to reward contributions of £500 with a toy rocket!

You also define a goal amount you're trying to raise and a timeframe in which you're trying to raise it, for example £5,000 within the next 30 days.

When your project page is ready, you publish it and hopefully lots of people will look at it. Some visitors will likely be people you've been contacting via marketing and outreach, while others could just be people who have been browsing the site.

Some of these people will really like what you're offering. They'll either like you and the project or they'll like the rewards – either way, they'll become **backers**, giving you money in exchange for the freebies. The site will store their credit card details, although at this point no money actually changes hands.

When the 30 days are up, one of two things will have happened. Either more than £5,000 will have been pledged to your campaign, in which case it's a success, or you will have fallen short of your target, which means you've failed.

If you've been successful, the backers' credit cards will be charged and you'll have to deliver the rewards you promised. The money collected is sent to you, minus the fees the site will charge you for using their platform and processing the credit card payments.

But if you missed your goal, no one's credit card is charged and you don't receive any money. Everyone goes back to where they were before the campaign started, except you've spent a lot of time and effort putting your campaign together.

This is the traditional crowdfunding model and it's called **all-or-nothing**, which is exactly what it sounds like. If you reach your goal, you get the money; if you miss, even by a few pennies, you don't get anything.

Some sites do offer a **flexible** funding model whereby, even if you fall short of your goal, you can still have the money that's been pledged, and we'll discuss these later in the book.

ESSENTIAL CROWDFUNDING CAMPAIGN ELEMENTS

Once you know you're going to crowdfund, you need to start planning the elements you'll need. The most basic elements of a crowdfunding campaign are:

- **A specific project.** Most sites want you to be able to say what the campaign is for, such as a film (or distribution of a film). It can't relate to ongoing or vague costs like 'helping me pay rent'. Your backers will want to visualise the final project and give money specifically to make that thing happen. The more detail you can give them during the campaign, the more likely they'll be to believe it's going to happen and therefore support you.

- **A fixed timeframe.** Crowdfunding campaigns normally happen with a strict time limit. Most campaigns allow for 30 days in which to raise the money needed, although you can choose a longer or shorter period of time.

- **A clear financial goal.** This is the amount you need to raise, especially important if you end up using an all-or-nothing platform (see above). Most sites let you over-raise, meaning that if you hit your target goal before the end of the campaign, you can keep it going until the time is up, collecting more than you intended. It's not uncommon for really popular projects to raise many times their original goal.

- **A team.** As we'll see, crowdfunding is a lot of work and you'll need people to support you. Often it's the same people who will become/ are the key creatives in your final film. The writer, producer, director, actors, etcetera, all have a stake in seeing the project get funded. Plus, there's no better way of proving you have an awesome team than to get them involved in the crowdfunding video and campaign. It allows your community to meet them and test their mettle.

Your team doesn't have to consist of the people physically around you. The vast majority of your crowdfunding activities will be online, so you could assemble a team from all over the world and use Skype, email and social media to coordinate and keep in touch.

- **A crowdfunding platform.** You need a central hub for your campaign where people can find out more about the project, see the rewards and actually donate money. Most people use sites designed to host crowdfunding campaigns, such as Kickstarter or Indiegogo, but you could build one yourself.

- **Rewards.** These are what your supporters get in return for giving you money. They can be physical, like DVDs or posters, digital, such as a PDF of the script or video download, or virtual, such as a tweet or credit on the final film.

- **Text and images for your pitch.** You're going to need to explain what you want to do, why, how much it'll cost, what you'll spend the money on and all the other details of your campaign.

- **A campaign video.** Strictly speaking this is optional, but campaigns with videos do a lot better than those without, especially for filmmaking campaigns. The video sits at the top of your campaign page, and is probably the thing most people will engage with when they first reach your page.

Throughout this book we're going to be looking at each of these elements in detail.

A BRIEF HISTORY OF CROWDFUNDING

Independent filmmakers have always had to look for new, innovative ways to raise money for their films, so when online crowdfunding started to become more organised, it quickly grew into a major source of independent film funding.

The oldest example we have of a filmmaker using online-based crowdfunding is Mark Kines, who raised $150,000 for his feature film *Foreign Correspondents* back in 1999. A few years later Franny Armstrong raised £1.5 million between 2004 and 2009 for her climate change documentary *The Age of Stupid*.

Then, around the late 2000s, we started to see larger platforms being established, enabling anyone to set up a crowdfunding campaign

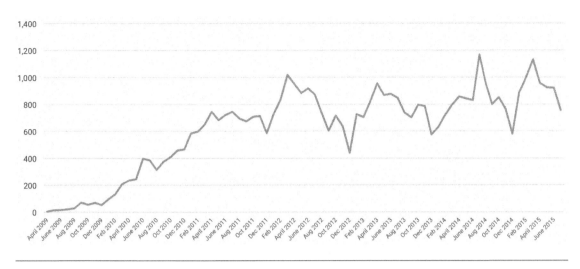

FIG 1.3 NUMBER OF KICKSTARTER PROJECTS LAUNCHED BY MONTH

in minutes. Indiegogo was slightly ahead of Kickstarter, but Kickstarter has become the largest and best known of all the platforms.

Within only a few years they had hosted 20,000 film campaigns and their numbers continue to increase. This can be seen in the data shown in Figure 1.3, which comes from my research into Kickstarter film projects and shows the number of projects launched every month over the last few years.

In recent years there have been ever-larger campaigns, the biggest of which to date was

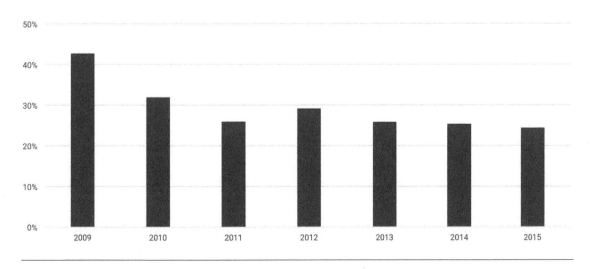

FIG 1.4 PERCENTAGE OF DOCUMENTARY PROJECTS ON KICKSTARTER

the Veronica Mars movie which raised almost $6 million on a target goal of just $2 million.

Now, crowdfunding is an established funding route for independent filmmakers and is used for all types of films.

CHANGES IN CROWDFUNDING FOR FILMS

Many things have changed in the seven years since Indiegogo kick-started the online crowd-funding boom for filmmakers.

Documentaries used to make up almost half of all film projects on Kickstarter but now account for about a quarter (see Figure 1.4).

The initial novelty and enthusiasm for crowd-funding has waned a little; most people in the filmmaking community have at some point experienced crowdfunding fatigue where too many of their Facebook friends have been promoting yet another film.

The quality and complexity of crowdfunding campaigns has increased. If you go back and look at early campaigns they seem relatively home-made and naive compared to the slick operations of today.

We're also seeing some of the biggest Hollywood companies and stars starting up crowdfunding pages, not always to a friendly reception online.

On the plus side, there are far more tools to help you plan and run your campaign. These range from getting the word out there to managing supporters and analysing how your project is doing.

SUCCESS RATE

The number of projects has increased dramatically, although, interestingly, the percentage that successfully reach their funding goal has stayed pretty static. Across all film projects between the

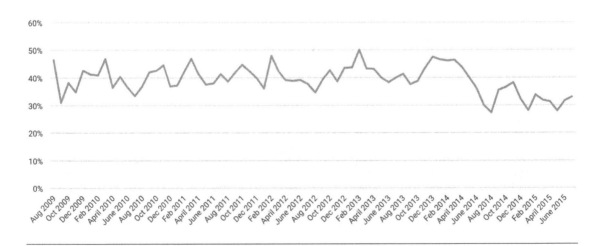

FIG 1.5 AVERAGE SUCCESS RATE OF KICKSTARTER PROJECTS

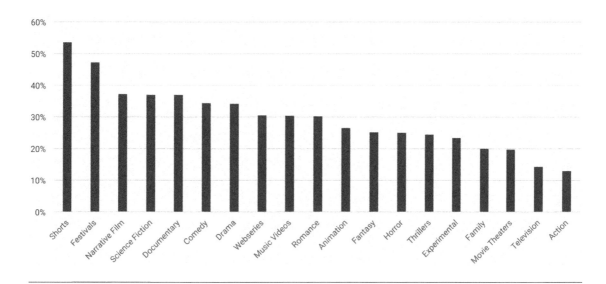

FIG 1.6 KICKSTARTER SUCCESS RATES BY TYPE OF FILM

start of Kickstarter and July 2015, the average success rate was 38% (see Figure 1.5).

Successes are not evenly spread across genres; some film project types have better completion rates than others.

As shown in Figure 1.6, short films have the highest success rate, with 54% reaching their goal. The least successful project types are action films and television shows, although this could be explained in part by the fact that the average short film goal is just $22,000, whereas the average action project is after $377,000 and TV shows ask for an average of $333,000.

THE ADVANTAGES OF CROWDFUNDING

Before you start, it's important to understand the best and worst sides of crowdfunding, so I've put together a list of 20 pros and 20 cons to try to give you an idea of all the aspects you need to consider before launching a campaign.

The advantages are as follows:

1. **List for free.** The vast majority of sites don't charge a listing fee, meaning there are no financial barriers to launching a campaign.

2. **Low fundraising fees.** Fees are around 5% of the money you end up raising, which is less than the cost of other forms of film finance.

3. **Minimal financial outlay.** You don't need much money to actually run a campaign. The only unavoidable costs are the fees charged by the sites and the cost of giving your backers the rewards you've promised them. However, you are in control of these; you can calculate what they'll be in advance and they only kick in if you're successful in raising the money.

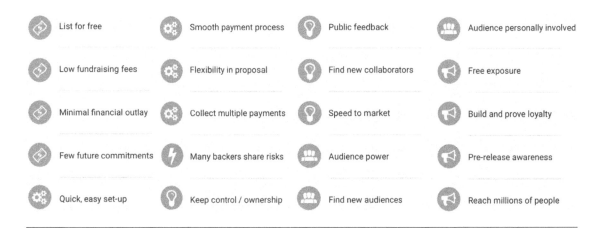

List for free	Smooth payment process	Public feedback	Audience personally involved
Low fundraising fees	Flexibility in proposal	Find new collaborators	Free exposure
Minimal financial outlay	Collect multiple payments	Speed to market	Build and prove loyalty
Few future commitments	Many backers share risks	Audience power	Pre-release awareness
Quick, easy set-up	Keep control / ownership	Find new audiences	Reach millions of people

FIG 1.7 THE ADVANTAGES OF CROWDFUNDING

4. **Few future commitments.** Crowdfunding doesn't burden you with future commitments. You'll need to deliver the rewards you've promised and send occasional updates, but beyond that you don't have any obligations once the campaign is over. Compare this to what traditional investors might require of you in the process of making or selling the film. With crowdfunding, you have no money to repay, no profits to share and no interest to pay.

5. **Quick and easy set-up.** The main crowdfunding websites are extremely user-friendly. They are designed to make it easy for you to set up a campaign and get going almost straight away.

6. **Smooth payment processes.** All payments are handled by the hosting platform so you don't have to worry about how you're going to charge credit cards or think about the issue of security when collecting people's financial details.

7. **Flexibility in proposal.** You have a huge amount of flexibility in what you can propose. This is twofold – flexibility in the types of film projects you can raise money for and flexibility in how you present your campaign. The film industry has a small number of types of films it's willing to fund. If you're making something more avant-garde or unusual you will struggle to get traction. Similarly, when it comes to presenting your projects to traditional funders, banks require business plans and investors want to see projected returns.

8. **Collect multiple payments.** By using an established crowdfunding platform there's no limit to the number of people you can take money from. The largest campaigns have tens of thousands of backers; if you had to manage the payments yourself, you might have to turn money away.

9. **Many backers share the risk.** When you have multiple backers they are sharing the

risks by each putting in tiny amounts of money. So, rather than having to convince one investor to give you $10,000, you can find 1,000 backers to give you $10 each. This allows riskier projects to get funding without having to water down their plans.

10. **Keep control/ownership.** This is a big one. You keep control and you keep ownership of the intellectual property you create. Backers don't own any of your project and they don't have a say in how you achieve it. You need to live up to the promises you've made during the campaign but they can be quite vague. If you want to sell it in a different way or make a sequel, you can because you are in control.

11. **Public feedback.** The public nature of crowdfunding means you may get a lot of feedback, which can be invaluable in improving your campaign and your final film. During the campaign you will be discussing your project, and so backers, fans or just passing readers may be able to help you identify weaknesses or add to your ideas.

12. **Find new collaborators.** You will be talking publicly about the film you want to make, which inevitably means some people will really connect with you and your journey. They may join the team for this project or for others in the future.

13. **Speed to market.** The speed of crowdfunding means your campaign might run for only 30 days before you get the money and are able to start your project. If you go through traditional funding routes it can take a long time to close the deal and for much of that time you will be uncertain if your project is actually going to happen or not. If you run a 30-day crowdfunding campaign, you can be certain that, in 30 days' time, you'll have an answer to the question of whether or not you're funded.

14. **Audience power.** Crowdfunding puts more power in the hands of the audience than ever before. In the past a small number of people decided which films got made, but now, if enough people want a project to happen, then it will.

15. **Find new audiences.** Running a successful campaign means you're going to be introduced to new communities and new audience members all over the world, both for your current project and future ones.

16. **Audience personally involved.** There are a number of ways your audience can get personally involved, including leaving a comment, promoting the campaign, giving feedback and, of course, actually donating money. It's so much more than the old idea of just buying a copy of the film – it's about being part of the process.

17. **Free exposure.** Major crowdfunding platforms allow your project to be seen by people who initially went to the site to back a different project but who are now browsing around. This can be especially powerful if you get featured as a Staff Pick or rank highly on their search algorithm.

18. **Build and prove loyalty.** If you manage to fund your feature film without the film industry, you may still want a traditional film

distributor to come onboard towards the end to take your film into cinemas or get a TV broadcast deal. With a crowd of existing supporters, you're able to prove that your film is popular and has a ready-made army of people willing to promote the release. This can really improve your chances of getting a deal with an otherwise sceptical distributor.

19. **Pre-release awareness.** Historically, movies only start to build their audience when they're close to release, but you'll have a huge head start as you'll already have an engaged, emotionally invested audience.

20. **Reach millions of people.** From your own bedroom or office you can put your project in front of millions of people all round the world. Your audience is really only limited by your marketing and the quality of your campaign. Many campaigns have 'gone viral' and ended up being in front of a lot more people than originally intended.

So, there you have 20 great reasons why you should use crowdfunding. But now let's take a look at the drawbacks, as it's important we go into the process with our eyes open.

THE DISADVANTAGES OF CROWDFUNDING

1. **It's a huge amount of work.** There is a common fallacy that crowdfunding is a quick, easy way to raise 'free money', but the truth is a little tougher. It's a grind. Campaigns need to be created, perfected, promoted, tweaked, managed and then completed by sending out rewards. This takes passion, dedication and quite a bit of time. What you are actually doing in a crowdfunding campaign is converting your time and passion into money. This means, if you want a lot of money, you need to invest a lot of time and passion.

2. **Lost in the crowd.** There are many films using crowdfunding, and even more projects go live each month, so there's a chance you'll get lost in the crowd. Simply setting up a Kickstarter page won't automatically lead to money coming in. Success with crowdfunding is down to having a big community behind you, having an effective marketing strategy or getting picked up and promoted by a larger community.

3. **Who you have to be.** Crowdfunding requires you to be a certain kind of outgoing, confident, social person. You need to be constantly in 'sales mode' and willing to ask everyone you've ever met for money. Some people might find this comes naturally while others will need to develop and hone these skills.

4. **New type of pitching.** Even if you're an experienced professional who is used to pitching movie ideas to executives or investors, you're going to need to learn a new style of pitching. Go to Kickstarter and watch as many videos as possible. You will see it's not just about telling the audience how good the story is; you have to pitch yourself and your own journey too.

5. **Creativity needed.** Your project has got to be clever or creative to really stand out. And then there's the actual pitch text, imagery and video: they need to be creative and

A huge amount of work	Cost of fees	Negative feedback	Unpredictable nature of film
Lost in the crowd	Other direct costs	Complaints and anger	Relationships not guaranteed
Who you have to be	Non-direct costs to you	Resentment at requests	Pestering your audience
New type of pitching	Damage your reputation	People may steal your idea	Hard to repeat
Creativity needed	Failure hurts future options	Risks for audience	Novelty is fading

FIG 1.8 THE DISADVANTAGES OF CROWDFUNDING

attractive. This takes good ideas, hard work and a high level of skill.

6. **Cost of fees.** Kickstarter and Indiegogo take 5% of what you raise, plus all transactions have a processing fee of around 3%. Later in the book we'll break these down so you can budget in line with how much of the money you raise you can expect to receive.

7. **Other direct costs.** As well as fees, there are other things you might need to spend money on. There are the rewards you're sending out to your backers and any other services you may use in creating the campaign, such as design or marketing.

8. **Non-direct costs to you.** You're likely to be working on this campaign for a month or two part-time and maybe the same again full-time. During this time you'll still have to eat, travel and pay the rent. These are the opportunity costs of what you're doing because you can't be anywhere else earning money.

9. **Damage to your reputation.** The nature of a crowdfunding campaign is very public, so if you make a misstep or are misinterpreted, you could receive negative attention.

10. **Failure hurts future options.** It's not the end of the world if your campaign fails, but it also doesn't look great in the future when you try other financing routes. Most of the major platforms keep old campaigns live; anyone can find your old project and see how far away from your goal you were. They do this for transparency, which is wonderful, but it does mean you can't delete the page and pretend it never happened. If you're unlucky, it could even be among the top entries in Google for you or your company.

11. **Negative feedback.** The internet is not the happiest place at times. So, if you're aiming to find hundreds or thousands of backers, you have to expect at least a few people to take a dislike to you or your project.

12. **Complaints and anger.** If there's a delay in your project, or you send out a T-shirt in the wrong size, some people will complain. Some people get angry quickly. So you could go out for the weekend and come back home on Monday to a whole flurry of angry people publicly and privately complaining to you.

13. **Resentment at requests.** You will have to ask a lot of people you've never met for money and support, and this will annoy a few people. I don't know about you but I have lots of filmmaker friends on Facebook and there are a few who seem to run a crowdfunding campaign every few months. It's frustrating to be tapped so many times for money.

14. **People may steal your idea.** You have to be very open for your crowdfunding to work, which means revealing parts of your film's awesome ideas, story or characters. This means someone could conceivably steal your ideas. If your film has a specific and unique concept, which is particularly fresh and powerful, then you may not want to reveal it before it's ready.

15. **Risk for the audience.** There are risks for the audience as well, as they're paying for something they may not receive for a while, if ever. Bear this in mind and do your best to gain their trust and therefore their support.

16. **Unpredictable nature of film.** Film is a massively unpredictable business, and delays are common. You could end up in a situation that's totally not your fault, but one in which your backers feel cheated or lied to. Most of your backers won't understand the unpredictability of the film industry and will expect you to still keep to your original plan.

17. **Relationships not guaranteed.** Just because you've reached a lot of people doesn't mean you've built a useful community. And even after you're funded, there's no automatic transformation of these backers into fans who'll be supportive of you in the future. You have to earn that all over again.

18. **Pestering your audience.** There's a fine line between keeping people abreast of your campaign and spam. And people you're communicating with may feel you've crossed that line.

19. **Hard to repeat.** Crowdfunding is hard to do twice. This is partly because it takes so much time, energy and passion, you may not exactly be chomping at the bit to go straight back into it. Also, if you've run a successful campaign, you've probably asked everyone you've ever met for tweets, messages and money; doing that again might be tricky.

20. **Novelty is fading.** In 2009 and 2010, crowdfunding was new, fresh and different. But the novelty has worn off. It can still work, but there's more competition and the overall standard of campaigns is higher.

WEIGHING UP THE ADVANTAGES AND DISADVANTAGES

To better show you where the opportunities and challenges lie, I've assigned each pro and con to a category according to the following definitions:

FIG 1.9 WEIGHING UP THE ADVANTAGES AND DISADVANTAGES OF CROWDFUNDING

- **Creativity.** These are responsibilities you'll have in generating interesting, creative and clever ideas in order for your campaign to stand out.

- **Risks.** These are the things that could go wrong or you could lose out on if you're unlucky.

- **Financial.** The financial pros relate to the money you might receive and the cons to what the campaign could cost you.

- **Marketing.** These are the activities you're going to have to do to get the word out there, attract an audience and convert them into backers.

- **Audience.** Not the people who will see your final film but those witnessing and backing the crowdfunding campaign.

- **Process.** This is the sequence of steps you'll need to take in order to launch and run your project.

The results of this are shown in Figure 1.9.

We can see that most of the advantages fall into the categories of audience, marketing, financial, creativity and process, while nearly all the negative aspects have to do with the risks inherent in crowdfunding.

You can minimise your risks by talking to other filmmakers who've run crowdfunding campaigns and by planning your campaign in as much detail as possible before you launch it. This means budgeting, scheduling, building a team, creating a marketing strategy and getting feedback – all aspects we'll examine in subsequent chapters.

HOSTING YOUR CAMPAIGN

In this chapter, I'm going to take you through a number of the major crowdfunding sites to help you decide which one to pick to host your campaign.

KICKSTARTER

This is the most commonly used crowdfunding site. It is the one people often use as shorthand: in the same way that to 'Google' something means to search for it, to 'run a Kickstarter' is synonymous with running a crowdfunding campaign.

Kickstarter was launched in 2009. They're currently based in New York and so far over ten million people have backed Kickstarter projects. One of their largest categories is Film and Video and they've hosted over 50,000 film projects to date.

They run on the all-or-nothing funding model, which means if you don't reach your goal in the allotted time, the backers don't have their credit cards charged and you get nothing.

One of the interesting things about Kickstarter is that in 2015 it became a 'Benefit Corporation', which means that while it is still a for-profit company, not a charity, it is legally obligated to consider its impact on society. This really shows the ethos of Kickstarter and how it is a commercial company but with community at its heart.

PROJECTS SUITABLE FOR KICKSTARTER

Kickstarter has various rules governing what kinds of projects are allowed to use the site:

- Projects must be single projects, like a film or TV series, which means you can't raise money to support the running costs of your company.

- You must have a clear goal, such as 'We need $2,000 to make this horror film', and they expect it to eventually be completed. You'll need to state an estimated delivery date for when the thing you're creating will be completed, regardless of whether it is virtual or physical.

- You're not allowed to fundraise for charities. Many other sites do allow that, but Kickstarter does not.

- You're not allowed to offer financial incentives, so you can't say that backers get a percentage of the profits or an ownership share in the company.

- The creators are liable for delivering their awards, not Kickstarter. What that means is that backers who pay for something and don't get it can't obtain a refund from Kickstarter. Kickstarter collects all of the money, takes off their fees and then gives what's left to you; that's the end of the relationship they have with the backers, meaning you are personally liable for delivering the rewards.

Within their 'Film and Video' category, there are a number of subcategories, including 'Action', 'Animation', 'Comedy', 'Documentary', 'Drama', 'Experimental', 'Family', 'Fantasy', 'Festival', 'Horror', 'Movie Theatres', 'Music Videos', 'Narrative Film', 'Romance', 'Science Fiction', 'Shorts', 'Television Thrillers' and 'Web Series'.

WHO CAN BE A CREATOR ON KICKSTARTER?

If you wish to create a project on Kickstarter you need to be over 18 and living in one of the countries listed in Figure 2.1. You also need to have an address, a bank account and some sort of ID in that country and a major credit or debit card.

Although only people in the countries listed in Figure 2.1 are allowed to run projects, anyone can back a project anywhere in the world. So your backers can come from countries not included on this list.

LOCATIONS OF KICKSTARTER PROJECTS

Kickstarter is quite focused on America, although less so than it has been in the past. In recent years they have made a real effort to try to expand internationally.

Figure 2.2 is based on my research into Kickstarter film projects. As you can see, in

FIG 2.1 LIST OF QUALIFYING KICKSTARTER COUNTRIES

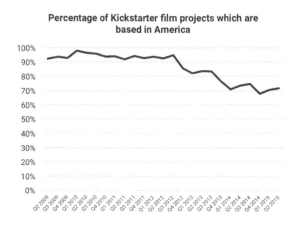

Percentage of Kickstarter film projects which are based in America

Country	Film projects		City	Film projects
USA	39,933		Los Angeles	7,093
UK	3,706		New York	3,380
Canada	1,185		London	1,567
Australia	576		Chicago	1,181
Germany	150		Brooklyn	1,135
France	149		San Francisco	922
Netherlands	118		Boston	668
Italy	109		Seattle	667
Mexico	105		Atlanta	658
India	94		Austin	632
Sweden	91		Portland	610
China	83		Philadelphia	497
152 other countries	1,886		4,128 other cities	28,519

FIG 2.2 LOCATION OF KICKSTARTER PROJECTS

summer 2009 94% of film projects were based in the US but by 2015 that had dropped to just 72%.

After America, popular countries are the UK, Canada and Australia. I think it's quite likely that we are going to see far more campaigns based in other countries as the years go on. So far I've found seven film projects based in Antarctica!

If we look at cities (right-hand side of Figure 2.2), we can see Los Angeles has the greatest number of Kickstarter projects, followed by New York, London and Chicago. These are known as some of the most creative cities in the world, so it's not surprising that's where many Kickstarter film projects are based.

FEES

As with almost all crowdfunding sites, Kickstarter charges fees for their work. If your project is successful they'll charge in three ways:

- 5% of the amount you raise is their fee.

- 3% of the amount you raise goes to credit card processing.

- There is also a small set figure per transaction depending which country your project is in (see Figure 2.3). There is a lower set fee for pledges below ten currency units (i.e. under $10 for US projects, £10 for British projects, etc.). These are around a third or a quarter of the set fees shown in Figure 2.3. (Note the 5% and 3% fees are the same for all amounts.)

As an example, if you raise $10,000 from 500 backers, you should expect to physically receive just over $9,000, which is 90% of the money pledged.

Later in the book we'll be looking at building budgets so you can get a clear idea of what to expect.

Note all of these fees are charged only if you actually reach your goal, because if you fail in the campaign no money changes hands.

If you're fortunate enough to be able to pick which country you're going to base your project

🇺🇸	United States	5% + 3% + USD $0.20	🇸🇪	Sweden	5% + 3% + SEK kr3.00
🇬🇧	United Kingdom	5% + 3% + GPB £0.20	🇩🇰	Denmark	5% + 3% + DKK kr3.00
🇨🇦	Canada	5% + 3% + CAD $0.20	🇳🇴	Norway	5% + 3% + NOK kr3.00
🇦🇺	Australia	5% + 3% + AUD $0.20	🇨🇭	Switzerland	5% + 3% + CHF Fr0.20
🇳🇿	New Zealand	5% + 3% + NZD $0.20		Netherlands, Germany, Italy, Austria, Spain, Luxembourg, France, Belgium and Ireland	5% + 3% + EUR €0.20

FIG 2.3 KICKSTARTER TRANSACTION FEES

in, because you have team members all round the world, take a closer look at the currency rates. Projects in New Zealand are currently only paying about 93% of what Danish creators have to pay.

INDIEGOGO

Indiegogo was the first big crowdfunding site, founded a year before Kickstarter, in 2008. They are based in San Francisco and say they have 15 million monthly visitors.

Film is one of their major categories, although they also run projects of other kinds. Their guidelines tend to be a little looser than Kickstarter's, and we'll see this later on in the book as we look at what is and isn't allowed.

They have two different funding models: **Fixed Funding** and **Flexible Funding**:

- The fixed funding model is the same as Kickstarter, also known as all-or-nothing. You set a goal and if you don't have enough pledges by the end of your campaign, you don't get any money.

- Flexible funding, on the other hand, lets you keep whatever money was pledged, even if you miss your goal amount. If you're trying to raise $10,000, but actually only raise $8,000, you have the option to still take that $8,000. In that case, you still have the same obligations to give your backers what you've promised them, e.g. T-shirts or DVDs.

Indiegogo have a clever referral scheme whereby you can give unique weblinks to people, which they then promote, allowing you to be able to tell who is driving traffic to your campaign. You can set up rewards for people based on their traffic numbers. It's a good way to reward people for having a positive impact on your campaign in a way other than giving cash.

Indiegogo call their rewards 'perks'. For ease I'm going to call them rewards, but if you do go with Indiegogo you'll need to remember that.

If you've received offline contributions, so someone you know physically has sent you $100, you'll be able to add that to the campaign to make sure they are listed as a backer, and that it adds towards your total, so people can see how much you're actually raising on and offline. They also have something neat which is a little short link, igg.me/at/whatever you want to put on your URL.

FEES

Indiegogo fees are the same as Kickstarter's. Before 15 July 2015, they had different fees for their fixed and flexible funding methods. Fixed funding projects had a 4% fee whereas flexible funded projects were charged at 9%. They moved on from that and now charge everyone 5%, the same as Kickstarter. I mention this in case you hear people or websites quoting the old fee structure.

They work with PayPal, major credit cards and ApplePay. Credit card transactions incur a 3% processing fee, plus 30 US cents. PayPal charges are a bit more complicated, but they are generally between 3% and 5%.

You have to be a bit careful if you're expecting to get a large number of backers from different countries because sometimes, especially if it's a smaller country, they might impose additional charges when transferring money to you. It's all laid out on the Indiegogo website, but is a little complicated. You don't necessarily have to run the campaign in your own currency, but projects in US dollars must have a US bank account.

When you finish your campaign and Indiegogo wire you the money, there will be an additional $25 wire fee.

SEED&SPARK

Seed&Spark was launched towards the end of 2012 and is based in Los Angeles.

They have a video on demand distribution platform, meaning you can run a crowdfunding campaign with them and then use their platform to deliver the final film to backers and sell it to other people. They sell short films for $0.99 and feature films for $2.99, with filmmakers receiving 80% of the revenue.

They use a flexible funding model, although you have to raise at least 80% of your target amount.

They have only run about 250 film projects to date but do claim a success rate of 75%, which is very high.

Their fees and processing fees are very similar to Kickstarter's and Indiegogo's, at 5% and around 3% respectively.

A nice little detail with Seed&Spark is that when backers get to the checkout they're asked if they want to cover the 5% fee on top of their donation. They estimate filmmakers receive about 95% of the money pledged, which, after taking processing fees into account, implies that half of the donors are actually paying the fees themselves.

They also allow you to request goods and services from your backers, so rather than asking for money you could say 'I need someone to lend me a camera for a week', or 'I need someone to let me into a location'.

Overall, I'd say they're really focused on improving the situation for independent filmmakers. They run educational events, training and publish a biannual magazine called *Bright Ideas*.

ULULE

Ulule is one of the biggest non-English-language crowdfunding sites. They say they are after creative, innovative or community-minded projects and obviously film falls into that.

They've hosted about 16,500 projects, raising about 40 million euros, and have a very high success rate. In 2015, their success rate was 70%.

They run an all-or-nothing funding model although you can choose whether your goal is a set amount of money (like Kickstarter) or a certain number of rewards being sold.

Their main focus is Europe so you need to have a bank account in one of the EU countries, Switzerland, Liechtenstein, Norway or Iceland.

Their fees are just over 6.5% when people pay via credit card, and just over 4% when using PayPal or cheque plus VAT at the local rate. They have lower rates for projects under 100,000 euros.

At the time of writing, the biggest film funded on Ulule has been a French movie that raised 681,000 euros on a goal of just 35,000, called *Noob, le Film!*

TUBESTART

Tubestart, which was started in 2013, is for film and video projects only and has an interesting rewards system.

First, they have 'Biddable Rewards', meaning you can set a minimum starting bid under which you aren't willing to sell your reward. And then whoever is the highest bidder at the end of the auction wins the reward.

Second, they have partnered with Spreadshirt and CafePress to offer 'Hands Free Rewards'. These are T-shirts, mouse mats and a whole host of other items you can sell as rewards, but which are printed and shipped by the partners, meaning you never have to touch the items. Once you've uploaded the designs everything is fully automated, which they call 'setup & forget'.

They have four funding models:

- Fixed Funding: a one-time project running for 30–90 days where you get paid only if you meet or exceed your goal (same as Kickstarter).

- Flexible Funding: a one-time project running for 30–90 days where you get paid all the money raised instantly, even if you fall short of your goal amount (similar to Indiegogo).

- Subscription Funding: an ongoing monthly subscription project where backers are given ongoing rewards as long as they're subscribed, or they can buy one-off rewards and you get paid instantly.

• Pledge Funding: an ongoing project where backers pledge to pay a certain amount every time you release a new video.

The standard fee is 4% although it's 8% if you use their flexible funding model and don't reach your target amount by the end of the campaign. They also have processing fees of around 3%.

POZIBLE

Pozible is Australian but also operates in China, the US and Singapore. They support creative projects and film is one of their largest categories. They run an all-or-nothing funding model.

In the past they've partnered with Screen-West (an Australian governmental body) to offer to match funding three to one on any money given for certain projects. So if someone gave a dollar, they would chip in a further three dollars.

They have a 63% success rate for Australian film projects, which is pretty high.

Their fees are 5% for projects raising under $100,000 US, 4% for projects raising between $100,000 and $500,000 US, and then finally 3% for projects raising over $500,000 US. The processing fees are about 2.5% plus 30 Australian cents.

They have a subscription option, meaning you can offer your backers a subscription to a video magazine. They also have a self-hosted option which allows you to run the campaign from your own website. This could be useful in keeping the traffic going once the project has been funded.

FUNDRAZR

FundRazr was established in 2010 and has raised over $69 million for over 45,000 campaigns (not all film projects, though). Their flexible funding model means you keep everything you raise, even if you've missed your goal.

American users can use PayPal or WePay, whereas international users have to use PayPal. Their fees are pretty standard: 5% plus a processing fee of just under 3%, plus 30 US cents.

FUNDANYTHING

FundAnything: they fund anything! You can do almost anything you want on there. It's open to people who want to run campaigns in the US, in the UK, Canada, Australia or anywhere in the Eurozone. Campaigns can last 30, 60 or 90 days.

They actually offer to refund donors if a project turns out to be false, which not all the sites do.

They charge 5% if you reach your goal and 9% if you don't. Their processing fees are around 3%.

Penn Jillett had a $1 million target for his movie funded on FundAnything. In the end he ended up raising $1.1 million.

ROCKETHUB

RocketHub was launched at the beginning of 2010 and is based in New York. They've got support from some political heavyweights such as Bill Clinton, and so they're helped by the US State Department to work in emerging regions of the world.

The fees are 4% if you reach your goal and 8% if you don't, plus processing fees of about 4%.

SLATED

Slated is quite different from a lot of the other crowdfunding sites we have looked at so far. It was specifically created for the film industry and aims to connect private investors with filmmakers. Unlike Kickstarter campaigns, which are rewards-based, Slated investors receive a financial stake in the film. This is the traditional film investment model but scaled up so you can reach lots of private investors in one place.

In 2014, Slated projects raised $322 million, and 65% of the films that sold at Sundance Film Festival in 2015 were made by Slated members. So they really do have an active and impressive user base.

When you create a project on Slated they will give you a 'package score', based on their opinion of various factors. They look at the strength and experience of the team, the quality of the project, and then make a judgement on the potential for financial returns. They then give you an overall package score and, obviously, the more attractive the package score, the more likely you are to get funded.

They have two types of members: investors and filmmakers. You have to be approved to be an investor. They do check your credentials and talk to you on the phone, and only approved investors can see the financial information on each project.

Unlike most of the other sites, you don't have to give a campaign deadline, although they do recommend doing that anyway as they think it's more likely to get people interested and involved in the project.

What they are essentially doing is acting as an intermediary between private investors and the filmmaker, but they don't actually process the money. So there are no fees and no credit card processing fees because they're not doing anything; they're just connecting people.

SEEDRS

Next we have Seedrs. This is equity crowd-funding for early stage businesses. They are a full investment platform, so they do actually handle the money and process it themselves; it's not just the introductions.

In this case you list your actual company, not a single film. This is the opposite of Kickstarter, which doesn't allow you to put companies on but does want projects. These guys aren't interested in individual projects – they're interested in selling shares in companies.

They are based in the UK and most of the work they do is in Europe.

Investors need to be verified by Seedrs and must be certified either as a 'high net worth individual', a 'sophisticated individual' or a 'professional client'. These are terms used by the Financial Conduct Authority in the UK, so not anyone can go on there.

Finally, they operate on an all-or-nothing funding model.

CROWDCUBE

Crowdcube is a UK-based crowd financing site where you can either sell shares in your company or issue mini-bonds as a way of borrowing money from investors.

They are authorised by the Financial Conduct Authority in the UK and most of the projects use the Enterprise Investment Scheme or Seed Enterprise Investment Scheme – EIS or SEIS. These schemes offer a way for high net worth individuals to invest in risky businesses and actually get a discount on their tax bill for doing so.

You'll need a business plan and financial forecast, so we're going back to the idea of private investors and the kinds of things you might be asked by a bank.

Their fees are 6.5% plus a £2,500 admin fee. It sounds like a lot, but for that they will set up your EIS or SEIS filing, issue share certificates

and provide other corporate services. So what you're getting here is a very different service from what you get at Kickstarter, which is why it costs a lot more.

BUILD YOUR OWN PLATFORM

One of the options you have is to build your own crowdfunding platform. Personally, I don't advise this because I think the negatives outweigh the positives. But there are many situations where, if you have the audience and the coding skills, it might perhaps work for you.

You'll need somewhere to host it, a website platform to make it run (such as WordPress) and a way of receiving and logging payments. These could be online payments (such as credit cards or PayPal) or offline (such as bank transfers, cheques or cash).

One of the challenges you'll face is letting people know your site exists. Kickstarter, Indiegogo and a lot of the other established sites will promote your campaign to their existing users, but you won't have this advantage if you build your own platform.

How you actually run it is up to you. You could be coding yourself and actually building all the elements separately or you could use an off-the-shelf platform. I've got a couple of examples below, but first let's look at the pros and cons of building your own platform.

PROS

• **You'll save on fees** because Indiegogo and Kickstarter charge you 5% of the money you raise as their fee. The processing fees will

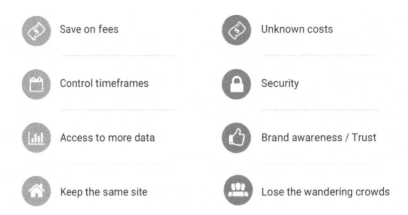

Save on fees	Unknown costs
Control timeframes	Security
Access to more data	Brand awareness / Trust
Keep the same site	Lose the wandering crowds

FIG 2.4 THE PROS AND CONS OF BUILDING YOUR OWN CROWDFUNDING PLATFORM

probably still apply for credit cards because they'll be charged by PayPal or whoever you're using to process cards (if collecting money via bank transfers, cheques or cash you may be able to avoid these fees).

- **You can control the timeframe.** One of the elements about these crowdfunding sites is that they put maximums and minimums on how long you can run your campaign for, so in the case of Kickstarter it's 60 days. You might actually want to have a longer campaign that coincides with a different schedule you have, such as a release schedule or events throughout the year. With your own platform you can control it all yourself.

- **You get a lot more information.** You do get data analytics from Indiegogo, Kickstarter, etc., but it isn't at the granular level of detail you could achieve if you managed to put something like Google Analytics on your website. That would give you far more detail about who is looking at your site. You would also have more access to your backers

because you'll be able to have their contact details in a way you don't get initially with Kickstarter. You can ask them questions about how they found you, etc., which could provide helpful information for tweaking your campaign as it goes on.

- **You can keep the same URL** on the site once it's funded and then convert that into the official site to promote or even distribute the film. The Kickstarter campaign you run will always be online and you can (and should) add updates to tell people how it's going, but it's not as exciting a year after the campaign is finished. Being able to use the same website, with the same URL, means all of the marketing you did before is still worth something. It's sending people to your site and you can still convert them from being backers into people who can help you with distribution.

CONS

- **There are a lot of unknown costs.** Unless you've run a site like this before it might be quite alien to think about calculating costs, e.g. how much a given plug-in or hosting is going to cost you. If there's a problem you're going to have to fix it, which might involve unexpected costs, such as bringing in a coder at the last minute because, say, your checkout isn't working. These kinds of things are all dealt with by the major sites without you even having to think about it.

- **Security is a major issue.** You're going to be collecting people's contact details and perhaps their credit card details. You have a legal and moral obligation to make sure these are secure. As we've seen in recent years, there has been an increasing amount of cybercrime where people hack into websites to get private data. If you do end up having a massively successful campaign on your site, which isn't as secure as some of the others, you could be seen as a weak target for data thieves.

- **People already trust Kickstarter and Indiegogo as brands.** They feel safe giving them their money and might feel it's okay to browse and shop the way they might at a major supermarket chain. However, when you create a whole new website and there is no brand association to instil that trust in people, they may be more wary about giving you money.

- **You won't have all the people browsing the site that Kickstarter and Indiegogo have.** You will start from zero traffic. You create a website, it goes up there, the world carries on. Nobody knows. To be fair, when you are using Kickstarter and Indiegogo you still have to assume that most of the traffic will be people you send there yourself, but there is still some passing trade you'll be missing out on when you build your own platform.

APPROACHES TO BUILDING YOUR OWN PLATFORM

There are at least three different ways you can build your own platform. As with all other mentions of products and services in this book, these are not recommendations as I've not road-tested each one.

WORDPRESS

The first is to use WordPress as the engine of your website (either installing it on your own site, or by using a wordpress.com domain) and use a combination of plug-ins and a special theme to make it look and function like a crowdfunding platform. See Figure 2.5 for some examples of these themes. WordPress is free and hosting can be very cheap (I use WPEngine).

OFF-THE-SHELF (PAID)

Next, you could pay more money and buy a whole system off-the-shelf. Rather than WordPress being the engine that's running the backend of your site, here a commercial platform will handle it instead. See Figure 2.6 for some examples of such platforms.

Some charge a one-off purchase price while others are on a monthly fee basis. This does away with some of the risks of unknown costs and the security risks we talked about earlier because, in theory, it's these companies that

37

www.fundifytheme.com

Buy for $99

FUNDER

c/o themeforest.net

Buy for $15

Unity

www.wpopal.com

Buy for $59

themes.skywarriorthemes.com/?
theme=Fundingpress

Buy for $59

c/o themeforest.net

Buy for $64

ignitiondeck

www.ignitiondeck.com

Buy for $79 - £449

FIG 2.5 EXAMPLES OF WORDPRESS THEMES YOU CAN USE TO BUILD YOUR CROWDFUNDING PLATFORM

CrowdfundHQ

www.crowdfundhq.com

Between $69 and $499 a month

crowdforce
power of the crowd

www.crowdforce.co

Between $499 and $999 a month

LAUNCHT

www.launcht.com

Set up fees plus $295 to $495 a month

**CROWD
VALLEY**

www.crowdvalley.com

Between $0 and $1,999 a month

crowdengine

www.crowdengine.com

Contact for pricing

investedin
We Power Crowdfunding!

www.invested.in

Between $345 an $999 a month

FIG 2.6 EXAMPLES OF OFF-THE-SHELF (PAID) SYSTEMS YOU CAN USE TO BUILD YOUR CROWDFUNDING PLATFORM

Selfstarter

www.selfstarter.us

MIT License

GeoTeo

github.com/Goteo/Goteo

GNU

Akvo

github.com/akvo

GNU Affero

GitTip

www.gittip.com

CC0 License

Spot.Us

github.com/spot-us/spot-us

GNU

Catarse

github.com/danielweinmann/catarse

MIT License

FIG 2.7 EXAMPLES OF OFF-THE-SHELF (OPEN SOURCE) SYSTEMS YOU CAN USE TO BUILD YOUR CROWDFUNDING PLATFORM

are processing your backers' cards, not you, and they know what they're doing.

OFF-THE-SHELF (OPEN SOURCE)

Finally, if you're hardcore and want to go for something really extreme but with a huge amount of control, and you have coding skills

(or know a friendly developer), see Figure 2.7 for some examples of open source crowdfunding platforms. You should really only go down this route if you know what you're doing as it's far from user-friendly. The advantage of this approach is that the platforms are usually free and allow you to customise every last detail to your own specifications.

PLANNING YOUR CAMPAIGN

In this chapter, I'm going to assume you've picked your platform and are ready to get cracking at building your campaign. Between this point and the launch, there are six areas you'll need to spend time in:

- Looking at the **online world of your potential audience**, understanding where they hang out, how they speak, what they like and a whole host of other details that will help you target your campaign to appeal to them.

- Getting to know **your chosen platform** so you can get the most out of the options open to you.

- **Reviewing past campaigns** from filmmakers who have completed (or are still on) the journey you're about to start.

- **Budgeting your rewards and campaign** so that you're confident you'll raise enough money to make your film if you reach your goal.

1	2	3	4	5	6
Online world and potential audience	Your chosen platform	Review past campaigns	Budget your rewards & campaign	Strategically build a team	Schedule your campaign

FIG 3.1 PLANNING YOUR CROWDFUNDING CAMPAIGN

- **Strategically building the team** of people who are going to come with you on the journey, providing skills, experience and support along the way.

- **Scheduling your campaign** so you're ready for what's to come and so that, during the most frantic moments of the process, you have things already prepared to allow you to focus on unexpected problems and opportunities.

QUESTIONS TO ASK YOURSELF BEFORE YOU START ANYTHING

Before you set out on the epic journey of building and delivering your crowdfunding campaign, there are a few questions you should ask yourself.

Is crowdfunding actually right for you?

Have a think about the cons mentioned earlier and make sure you're prepared for them. It will take a certain type of dedication and willingness

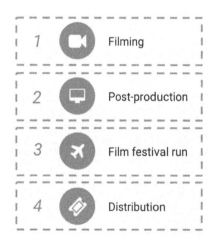

FIG 3.2 BREAKING YOUR CAMPAIGN INTO FOUR PARTS

to constantly pitch, promote and push your project on a large number of people. While I believe everybody can do what's needed, not everyone actually wants to.

Can you dedicate enough time and passion to see it through?

Your campaign will take up a lot of your time that would otherwise be spent on other work projects, on having fun or relaxing. This may be something you need to discuss with your nearest and dearest, as it may be you'll be using time you would otherwise spend with them.

Is your film 100% ready to be made once it's funded?

I don't mean 'Is the script 90% of the way there?' or 'Are you sure you can polish it before the shoot?' – I mean, is it 100% ready **now**? This is important for two reasons:

1. If your project isn't ready, this might become obvious during the process of putting it out there and showing it to potential backers. And if people spot flaws in what you're proposing, they could leave comments on the page or on social media that could harm your ability to fund the project.

2. Second, by setting up a campaign and publicly putting a timeframe in place, you are promising to deliver certain rewards by a certain date. If your project isn't ready, you could miss certain key dates when it comes to delivering rewards or the final film, which will anger your backers and cause you to garner negative attention.

Should you run a single campaign or a series of campaigns?

One of the things we are seeing increasingly is the breaking up of films into multiple campaigns. So, instead of running one large campaign to cover production, post-production, film festivals and distribution, you split it into four much smaller campaigns.

There are a number of reasons you might wish to consider this:

- If you manage to build an active community of backers who see you have delivered each time, it could create a snowball effect that allows you to leverage the success of one campaign to improve your odds on the next one.

- You'll be able to apply things you've learnt on early campaigns to the later ones.

- It enables you to be more specific when you are asking people for money, as you can say what every penny will be spent on. You can't do that in a single campaign as you aren't sure what will happen at the film festival or distribution stages.

- You can offer more tailored rewards, such as joining the filmmakers at the San Francisco Film Festival party. You wouldn't have enough information to be able to offer a reward like that at the very start of the project.

THE 5 P'S OF PRE-LAUNCH CROWDFUNDING

There is a lot of work to do in the 'pre-launch' phase and I've divided this into five categories (summarised in Figure 3.3):

1. **Pitch.** You're going to need to work out what your pitch is. This is a unique, compelling idea about why people should fund or promote your project.

2. **People.** This refers to the people you want to reach and are aiming to convert into backers. The pitch and the audience have

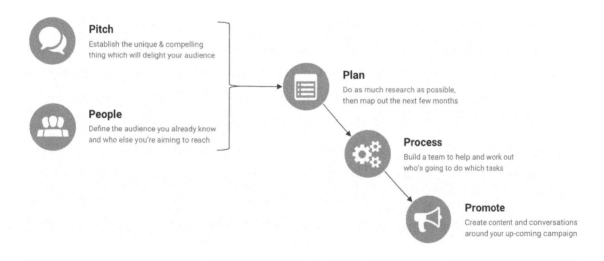

Pitch
Establish the unique & compelling thing which will delight your audience

People
Define the audience you already know and who else you're aiming to reach

Plan
Do as much research as possible, then map out the next few months

Process
Build a team to help and work out who's going to do which tasks

Promote
Create content and conversations around your up-coming campaign

FIG 3.3 THE 5 P'S OF PRE-LAUNCH CROWDFUNDING

to be worked out simultaneously as each informs the other. You may already know your pitch, so you need to think about which types of people would be most receptive to hearing it. Conversely, you may already have an audience of people in mind, so your challenge is to tailor your pitch to them.

3. **Plan.** You need to go through all the steps in this book, along with doing as much research on previous crowdfunding campaigns as possible. Then you're able to plan all the aspects of your campaign, including the text, images, videos and messages, as well as budgets and schedules.

4. **Process.** You need to create a process for achieving your plan by building a team of people to support you and signing up for all the services and third party companies you want to use.

5. **Promote.** Finally, you'll need a marketing strategy. Just having a crowdfunding page won't lead to money rolling in. However, if you have a strong pitch and clearly defined audience, it will be straightforward to build a marketing plan that gets your ideas in front of the right people.

THE IDEAL CAMPAIGN

The ideal crowdfunding campaign:

- **Brings something new to the table.** There's a fresh way of seeing the world or a unique mix of story elements to your pitch.

- **Has got to be fun to engage with.** Most people realise they can have a quicker and easier shopping experience on Amazon than on Kickstarter. So, part of the reason they choose to support crowdfunding campaigns is because they're fun. Via your marketing you may be able to catch people's attention for a few seconds, and if you entertain them enough in those few seconds, they might give you some more time and eventually some money.

- **Builds trust in the team and viability of the project you're proposing.** You're basically asking people to give you money on a promise that you'll make the final film and that it'll be worth watching. That's a big ask and all they have to go on is what you say in your text, images and video. But with the right tone and details, you can convince people you're worth taking a punt on.

- **Has a huge mass appeal while also feeling specific and personal.** If your core audience is six people in Utah, I don't hold out much hope of your ever getting funded. However, if you're appealing to a common human desire, in theory there are millions of people who could be converted from viewers into backers. But if you do this at the expense of sounding like real people, you could lose them. No one would support a crowdfunding campaign run by Coca Cola, or Starbucks, so you must be careful to keep that human touch. Every campaign will require a different compromise to achieve this.

- **Needs to give your backers very clear benefits.** People don't give money for your benefit; they do it for themselves. They want the rewards, or they want to feel good about supporting you. Simply stating you need money doesn't give people any reason to back you.

REASONS PEOPLE GIVE TO CROWDFUNDING CAMPAIGNS

Following on from the final point in the ideal campaign list, let's look at the main reasons people give money to crowdfunding campaigns:

1. **They want you to succeed.** They either know you or you've made such a good impression in your campaign that they're happy to chip in some money to help you reach your goal. This is the reason your friends and family give you money: they love you and want to see you succeed.

2. **The backers want to be part of something.** There is deep human desire to be part of something bigger than ourselves and it's what drives much of the social world, online and offline. As you build your community of donors, others may want to be part of it and join in the exclusive fun.

3. **They want to see the project happen.** This may be the case when you're doing a charity film or documentary. They feel the topic being tackled is important and want more people to know about it.

4. **They might want the end result of what you're making.** They want to view the film or own the product you are developing. Which means their donation is really a form of pre-selling where they're paying you now for something they will receive later down the line. This is how most crowdfunded technology products are pitched. It's essentially a shop with a very long lead time to delivery.

5. **They might want the rewards you're offering.** When you set up your campaign you state what items or services you're offering to people who donate. And people might say, 'Yes, I want that T-shirt or DVD.'

These reasons are summarised in Figure 3.4. On the left we have increasingly emotional reasons whereas the ones on the right are more transactional. You'll need to think carefully about your audience and decide what kinds of things will motivate them. Then build rewards that speak to their individual reasons.

FIG 3.4 REASONS PEOPLE DONATE TO CROWDFUNDING CAMPAIGNS

SETTING YOUR CAMPAIGN LENGTH

Another thing you're going to have to decide with your campaign is how long you're going to run it for.

HOW LONG CAN YOUR CAMPAIGN LAST?

- On Kickstarter, Indiegogo and Pozible you can run a campaign that runs for up to 60 days. The Kickstarter maximum used to be 90 days but they've since reduced that.

- Ulule say between 1 and 90 days.

- Seed&Spark only give you three options: 30, 45 and 60 days.

- RocketHub is between 30 and 75 days.

- Slated doesn't require you to set a time limit, although they recommend you do.

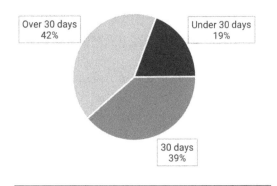

📅 Campaign lengths (days)	
Kickstarter	1 – 60
Indiegogo	1 – 60
Pozible	1 – 60
Ulule	1 – 90
Seed and Spark	30, 45 or 60
Rocket Hub	30 – 75
Slated	Optional

FIG 3.5

FIG 3.6 CAMPAIGN LENGTH OF KICKSTARTER FILM PROJECTS

If you're thinking of using a different platform from the ones listed here, read the small print to find out their campaign-length rules.

The most common campaign length on Kickstarter is over 30 days and it's how long most people presume a crowdfunding campaign will last.

A fifth of Kickstarter campaigns run less than 30 days and a handful of projects have run one-day, 24-hour blitz campaigns. That's terrifying, but if you feel you have a large enough community and a small enough goal, it might not be too hard to do.

HOW LONG SHOULD YOU CHOOSE?

Your initial reaction might be to make your campaign run for as long as possible to increase the time backers have to contribute. However, as we've already discussed, running a crowdfunding campaign takes a lot of time and energy, so you might want to focus on a shorter period of time.

Also, longer projects tend to have lower success rates. This may seem counterintuitive but it's because people can put more time and energy into actually pushing the audience to contribute if there's more urgency to the campaign. The one exception to this is when there's a really large goal; if you're trying to raise millions of pounds, it really will take time to create a movement and a community behind you.

Indiegogo say campaigns that run for less than 40 days are 6% more likely to reach their goals than those that run for longer than 40 days.

Ultimately, how long you run your campaign for is down to how long you can sustain it and keep the energy going.

Figure 3.7 summarises the research I performed on the success rate of Kickstarter film projects, split by their target goal and how long the campaigns ran for:

- For campaigns trying to raise **under $5,000**, the ones lasting under 30 days had a 62% success rate. Around half those lasting 30 days and 48% of those lasting over 30 days were funded.

- The success rate of projects raising **between $5,000 and $25,000** was lower overall, as you'd expect, but the pattern is the same, with short campaigns faring better.

- As the goal increases to **between $25,000 and $100,000** we see less of a difference.

- For projects **over $100,000** the success rate is highest for projects over 30 days, at 7.6%.

BUDGETING

One of the most important things when planning your campaign is the budget. In fact, there are two budgets you need to create: one for the final film you're making and one for the crowdfunding campaign. I'm going to assume you've budgeted for your final film already, so you know how much you'll actually need to make it.

RUNNING A CAMPAIGN ENTIRELY WITHOUT COST

Technically, it's possible to run a crowdfunding campaign for zero money because there are no charges for listing your project and you only pay fees once you have some backers giving you money.

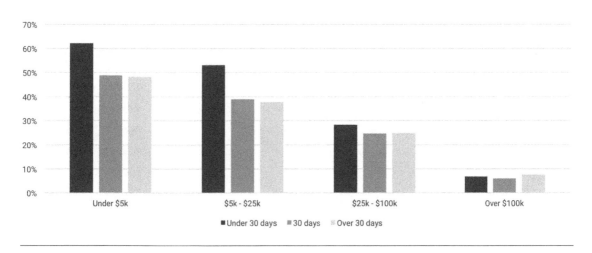

FIG 3 7 SUCCESS RATE OF KICKSTARTER FILM PROJECTS

However, you may find that if you don't spend any money:

- You can't reach enough people or the right people, so you've got a great campaign but it's being ignored in the pits of Kickstarter hell.

- It might be that your campaign doesn't look as slick or exciting as you need it to be because, even though you're amazing at crafting stories, you're lacking in Photoshop skills.

- You may not be able to take advantage of great opportunities you're offered, such as very cheap access to big communities.

Don't forget the costs of basic survival, such as food, travel and rent. I don't suggest listing these in the crowdfunding campaign budget, but you do need to make sure they're covered somehow.

You should also consider your time. Anything you do to further your campaign will be at the opportunity cost of other paid work. Also, you have a finite amount of time, so even if you're skilled enough to perform every task, you might not physically be able to.

THE TYPES OF COSTS YOU SHOULD CONSIDER

Let's take a look at what types of costs could be involved. I've grouped them into four different categories.

1. **Set-up**
   Although it's free to launch a project, you might need to spend money on photography, filming your campaign video or post-production work to make it look and sound better.

2. **Marketing**
   - You might choose to build a mailing list to get the word out there, for which you may need to pay a service like Mailchimp, Aweber or Mailflow.

   - You might want to subscribe to services that allow you to track the social media impact, such as which tweets are working, which Facebook posts are getting the most action, etc. This allows you to learn and double down on what's working.

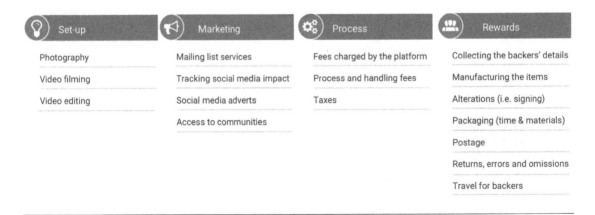

Set-up	Marketing	Process	Rewards
Photography	Mailing list services	Fees charged by the platform	Collecting the backers' details
Video filming	Tracking social media impact	Process and handling fees	Manufacturing the items
Video editing	Social media adverts	Taxes	Alterations (i.e. signing)
	Access to communities		Packaging (time & materials)
			Postage
			Returns, errors and omissions
			Travel for backers

FIG 3.8 THE COSTS YOU SHOULD CONSIDER WHEN BUDGETING FOR A CROWDFUNDING CAMPAIGN

- You might also want to use targeted Facebook advertising to reach new audiences. We'll go through that later in the book.

- You may have to pay for various ways to access communities. For example, you may need to pay to give a talk at a certain event, or to do advertising on a certain community platform, or it might be as simple as taking the admin from a certain site out for dinner, as that's how you're going to convince them to support your campaign.

3. **Process fees**

- These are the fees charged by the platform you're using, plus any money they charge you for handling credit card payments.

- Depending on your situation and the local laws, you may also be subject to taxes. For example, if you're a business in the UK that's turning over more than £85,000 a year, you have to charge VAT at 20%. So, if you give a backer a DVD in return for a £100 donation, you may have to hand £20 to the UK taxman.

4. **Cost of the rewards**

- Many first-time crowdfunders are burnt by underestimating the costs of the rewards.

- If you have a large number of backers, you may not be able to manage the collection of people's details yourself. Kickstarter does allow you to send a survey out to everyone who's contributed, but that doesn't give you the kind of advanced features an external company like BackerKit can. They charge a few hundred dollars to set it up and take 1% of the money you've raised.

- You need to create the physical rewards, as well as paying any costs for the creation of virtual or downloadable goods.

- If you've agreed to personalise or sign items, that can take time and money.

- In terms of postage and packing around the world, most sites let you set different delivery prices for different parts of the world.

- Some rewards will arrive broken, be sent to the wrong address or be the wrong items. You'll need to be able to handle returns and replacements.

- If you're offering rewards like attending a premier or party or having a part in the film, you'll need to be clear who's covering related costs. For example, when Zach Braff offered a part in *Wish I Were Here* for $10,000, it didn't include any travel, hotel or living expenses – the backer had to cover that themselves on top of their original donation.

AN EXAMPLE CAMPAIGN

Let's have a look at the mathematics of a simple Kickstarter campaign.

Say you need £8,000 to make your film, so you set up a Kickstarter campaign and offer the five rewards shown on the left-hand side of Figure 3.9. They range from being able to watch the film online when it's finished for £10, right up to being in the film if they give you £1,000 or above.

You run your campaign and get a total of 169 backers, divided between the rewards as shown in Figure 3.9. When you add this up,

	Reward	Backers	Gross	Processing	Cost each	Total cost	Net income
£10	Watch the film online	25	£ 250	£ 12.50	£ -	£ -	£ 237.50
£30	Above + DVD of the film	115	£ 3,450	£ 126.50	£ 5	£ 575	£ 2,748.50
£100	Above + DVD, poster and stickers	18	£ 1,800	£ 57.60	£ 18	£ 324	£ 1,1418.40
£300	Above + Credit on the film	9	£ 2,700	£ 82.80	£ 25	£ 225	£ 2,392.30
£1,000	Above + Be in the film	2	£ 2,000	£ 60.40	£ 25	£ 50	£ 1,889.60
		169	£ 10,200	£ 339.80		£ 1,174	£ 8,686.20

	Kickstarter Fees
5%	Kickstarter fee
3%	Payment processing fee
£0.20	Payment processing cost

Minus 5 %Kickstarter fee of £510.00
means you've raised **£8,176**

FIG 3.9 THE MATHEMATICS OF A SIMPLE KICKSTARTER CAMPAIGN

you find you've raised just over £10,000 – congratulations! But after all the fees and costs, will you have enough to make your £8,000 film? Let's have a look.

First, you need to take off the processing fees charged on credit cards. In this example they come to £440.

Next, you need to consider the cost of creating the rewards. The cheapest reward doesn't have a direct cost because I'm assuming it's a really simple set-up like a Vimeo password you just email everyone. A DVD costs you £5 to make, the bumper pack is £18 and the final two tiers cost £25, because you're sending them a tote bag as well.

Add that together and you have a manu-facturing bill of £1,174, leaving you with a net amount of £8,686.

The last thing to remove is Kickstarter's fee, which is 5% of the amount raised. In this case it's £510 as that's 5% of £10,200.

You needed £8,000 for your film and you've made it – just! But you can see how you needed to raise almost an extra quarter on top of the original goal to cover all the costs. Keep in mind your campaign may have different economics to this one, so you can't use this as a rule of thumb.

HOW TO CREATE A BUDGET FOR YOUR CAMPAIGN

Start by defining the rewards you're going to be offering. Then get quotes from as many suppliers as you can. Look at the difference between doing some of the work in-house (such as using a local T-shirt supplier and posting them yourself) and using a drop-shipping company that does it all for you, which will cost more but might make sense financially.

Look at how much postage costs to all areas of the world, taking into account the size and weight of your reward packages. Make a note of delivery estimates as you'll need to communicate to your backers how long they should expect to wait, once the campaign is funded, before receiving their rewards.

Err on the side of caution and if you have two prices you're considering, budget for the more expensive one.

For each reward bundle, check the costs for that combination. You might know what it costs to send a T-shirt and DVD separately, but, if you're offering them in a combo, it could affect the postage costs.

Look at the profit margin on each reward. If they differ greatly, you won't know how much you're going to raise until the campaign is over. Imagine you have two rewards priced at £10 – a T-shirt and a DVD. The T-shirt costs you £6 to create and ship and the DVD just £2. If you raise your money entirely from backers claiming the T-shirt, you'll make far less money than if everyone picked the DVD.

When someone claims a reward, they give Kickstarter their credit card details but the card is not charged until the campaign is over (and only if it was successful). This could be weeks later, during which time the card has been lost, stolen or overdrawn. So assume that a small number of your pledges will bounce. In this situation Kickstarter gives the backer seven days to fix the problem, after which their pledge is cancelled.

Take into account sales tax or VAT. Also, some countries have restrictions on what can be sent in or out of the country, so research what's allowed. For example, it's illegal to send a Kinder Egg to America, so best not to offer them as rewards!

The moment your campaign ends, you'll want to be sending out your rewards, but you may not receive the money you've been pledged for some time. For example, Indiegogo says it can take up to 15 business days to actually send you the money after the campaign closes. If you've not got any spare cash, you'll have to wait for that before you place the order with the T-shirt company or whoever is making your rewards. Then you'll have to wait for them to be delivered before you can pick, pack and ship them to backers. These delays could undermine the goodwill you've built up with the audience. If you have no choice but to do this, make sure it's clearly explained when the backers should expect to receive their rewards.

Finally, don't go overboard with spending on your campaign. Everything you spend is eating into the money you have to make your final film, which makes it that little bit harder to actually meet your target goal (or necessitates increasing the goal itself, adding further to the difficulty of the campaign).

Try making a smaller budget and see how it would work. Personally, I find the process of forcing yourself to cut costs on paper can sometimes help you see where you're overspending.

With an idea of how much your final film will cost, added to the costs of running your campaign, you should be getting close to setting your target goal. Now, let's sense-check it against other Kickstarter projects. Have a look for similarly budgeted projects on Kickstarter and see if yours is on a suitable level.

Figure 3.10 shows the average goals of all Kickstarter film projects between the start of 2009 and summer 2015. As you can see, action, TV and horror projects tend to have the largest goals. On the low end, web series, short films and music videos commonly ask for the least. The average short film goal is $22,000 and they have a 54% success rate, whereas the average TV show asks for $333,000 but only 14% are funded.

As the budgets increase, so the success rate drops, as shown in Figure 3.11. Over half of the projects trying to raise $1,000 are successful, compared with just 11% of those asking for over $50,000.

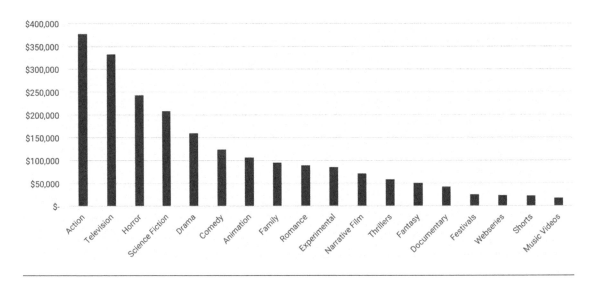

FIG 3.10 AVERAGE GOALS OF KICKSTARTER FILM PROJECTS BETWEEN THE START OF 2009 AND SUMMER 2015

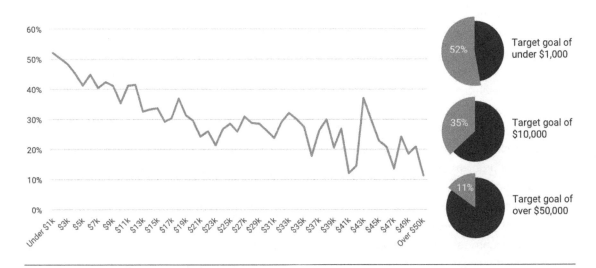

FIG 3.11 SUCCESS RATES OF KICKSTARTER FILMS

DEFINING YOUR AUDIENCE

Let's start thinking about who your audience will be.

You don't necessarily need a big audience, but you will need them to be motivated so that, at the very least, they'll be willing to listen to your pitch. Hopefully they're also going to give you some money, and share your campaign.

Having a large number of people who 'kinda like it' is less valuable than having a small number of people who really love it and are motivated to do something.

You've got two audiences to consider:

• Your existing audience; the people you know and who are around you

• Your potentially new audience; the people who have never heard of you and don't know anything about your project, but who you'll be able to reach through creating a campaign and marketing it

So, the first question is: is your existing audience big enough to fund your project on its own? If it is, great; focus on that audience. You know them, they know you, and this should really reduce the amount of brand-new marketing you need to do.

(Consider this – if you already know who makes up your audience, maybe you don't actually need crowdfunding. Crowdfunding platforms will charge you 5% plus handling fees, plus you have to send out rewards and things like that. Maybe you can reach your audience directly by creating your own website or just contacting them through other methods? That will save you time and money and allow you to be far more personal.)

If not, then, like most filmmakers, you'll need to branch out and reach new people. This new audience consists of people who wouldn't automatically donate, so you'll need to give them reasons to back you (compared to your friends and family, who may already have all the reasons they need).

Do research and chat to people who fall into your ideal target audience. What will get them interested in the first place and what will tip them over to donating? These could be different aspects of your campaign. It might be that the strong, funny hook you have will get them to the page, after which they need the promise of solid, physical rewards to get out their wallets.

Start by researching the communities and talking to them. Spend some time reading their posts on Facebook, Tumblr, Twitter, etc. and try to see the world from their point of view. There is no harm in putting out a message saying 'Hey, I'm going to be running a crowdfunding campaign, I think you guys are going to like it, but can I have some feedback first?' And then you post some ideas about it to test the waters.

Figure 3.12 shows some research I performed on Kickstarter film projects. As you can see, you don't necessarily need many backers to achieve your funding goal.

Only a small number of the people you appeal to will actually back you. So, how big does your initial audience need to be? Obviously, you want it to be as big as possible, but if you try and go for a huge audience, you might spread yourself too thin, meaning you don't really get anyone motivated or are too broad in your marketing.

The fewer other crowdfunding projects you can find appealing to that topic the better. If you're lucky enough to be appealing to a broad audience who've never been approached with a

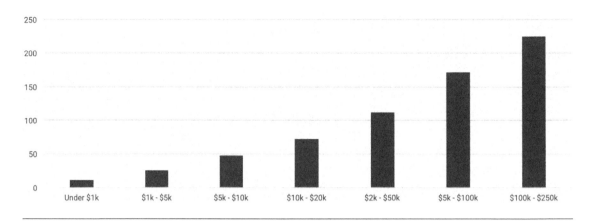

FIG 3.12 NUMBER OF BACKERS NEEDED TO REACH KICKSTARTER FUNDING GOALS

crowdfunding campaign, you may have novelty on your side. However, I suspect there are not many topics where this applies. (It's a good idea to go to Indiegogo and Kickstarter to look for campaigns on your subtopic. If there are a relatively small number, or a large number coupled with high success rates, you could be into a good subtopic.)

You might find you need to subdivide the first audience group you think of in order to be more specific. If your film is about astronauts, appealing to everyone interested in science would likely be too broad, whereas focusing on rocket enthusiasts might give you a more motivated audience. But is it a big enough audience? There are a few things we can do to find out.

RESEARCHING YOUR AUDIENCE ON FACEBOOK

Facebook advertising is a great way – in fact, probably the best way – to find data on the size of audiences around your topic.

It's free to use, so go to facebook.com/ads and then create an advert (you don't have to launch it, just create it). The options you have are shown in Figure 3.13. You can define your audience by a whole host of demographic criteria, and what topics they're into. Facebook then tells you roughly how many people fit the criteria you specified.

In this case there are four million adults in the UK who like horses. This is quite a broad group so I could use this tool to tweak my criteria and find a smaller audience which would likely be more motivated. Once I have these groups defined I can go on to relevant pages and see how big they are and how many people are engaging with them. Join the pages so you get a feel over the next few weeks of what they're saying. It'll also make it easier to contact people later on.

Prioritise the big pages, the personal pages and the active pages:

- The **big pages** are self-explanatory: the ones with the largest number of likes.

FIG 3.13 RESEARCHING YOUR AUDIENCE ON FACEBOOK

- The **personal** ones are where there is a single person who is speaking from their experience. These people are often called 'tastemakers'. They can be really useful in convincing other people your project is good and one they can trust.

- Lastly there are **active** pages: the ones that have a lot of people commenting, sharing and liking the posts put out there.

You want to look and sound as much like your audience as you can while still being true to yourself and your project. Reading these pages can be really useful in working out which side of yourself to put across first.

TWITTER AND INSTAGRAM

You can also try doing research and marketing via Twitter. Find key people around your theme and use tools like SocialBro or Rival IQ to understand more about that audience. Look at who is following these big people (or who the big people themselves are following) and see how active these people are in communicating.

Do they recommend other projects? You can look at someone's timeline to see if they seem to promote their own projects, in which case you will likely need to get them onboard at an early stage to have them promote yours as well.

Look for tweets which motivated the audience to retweet and comment. It might be that people like talking about horses, but it's only when they get to talk about how to look after horses that you get lots of people actually sharing and commenting. This will help you learn the kinds of language and subtopics that inspire action.

Instagram can also be quite useful. It can help you with the visuals, answering questions like: what are the common themes within the images on your topic and, also, how professional are they? Some topics will want very glossy, sexy, heavily graded, beautiful images, where others seem to prefer real, raw, human emotion.

PREPARING TO REACH YOUR AUDIENCE

Write down the audience group you think you can attract. Try and subdivide them so they are motivated and small; you can tailor your campaign to these people.

For the audience you already have links to, start building contact lists of the people who might be useful. Do this not just for people you know but for the whole team.

There's an old saying that goes 'Ask for money, get advice, ask for advice, get money'. What this means is that if you go to somebody and say 'Hey, please can I have some money?', what you're going to hear is 'You know what you should do...?', and then they're going to give you some advice. Instead, try saying to them 'Hey, can you help me with this, I'd love to get your feedback'. One of two things might happen: they give you great feedback, like the campaign and ask if you're looking for backers, or they don't like it and give you feedback that changes it into something they do like, after which they are much more likely to feel involved and hence to back the campaign.

So, early on, when you're testing your audience and starting to build links, don't go around saying 'I'm going to be asking you for money in three weeks'. Ask people for advice; open up and ask them to criticise your plan and give you feedback, because the worst outcome here is you get some useful pointers. The best-case scenario is that you bring people on to the team who are motivated and emotionally connected, or you find people who are ready to donate from the day you launch the campaign.

Later, when the campaign is actually running, these people will feel particularly included because they were there during the early days. They will be especially useful in getting other people involved.

Remember that your story starts from the moment you contact people. So make sure that what you're discussing relates to the actual campaign. There is a fine line, though. You don't want to go to these people and say 'I have no idea what I'm doing, please tell me what you want me to do'. At the same time, you're going to want to use these people's feedback to perfect your campaign.

BUILDING A COMMUNITY

How do you turn an audience into a community?

Remember to reply to people who connect to, comment on or back your campaign:

- First, be a nice person – say 'thank you'.

- Second, ask them how they found you. This is an easy way to start a conversation with people, but it's also useful information. If you find one of the smaller sites that you've been undervaluing is sending you most of your backers, maybe you'll need to focus more of your campaign on them.

- Finally, ask them to spread the word. Whether they've given you money or not, it might be more valuable to you to have people sharing your campaign.

Champion the people who support you on social media. When someone gives you money, say

'Hey, thank you so much for that, that was a really good thing'. It makes them feel good so that they're more likely to help further on. It also reminds your audience that people are backing and helping your campaign.

Bear in mind that, if it's a private donation, they might not want you to shout about it. With this in mind, you might want to send them a message saying 'I really want to thank you and I'm going to mention you on the Twitter feed, so let me know if that's OK'.

Generally, the more places you're promoting your campaign, the better. However, you can't be everywhere at once. Consider where you can actually be active. Much of this should be worked out from where your target audience spends most of its time; this will allow you to create a hierarchy of sites:

- At the top you have your actual crowdfunding page, whether it's Kickstarter, Indiegogo or whatever else you're using.

- Secondary from there will be a small number of key social networks feeding into that. You really want to use these to drive traffic. Facebook and Twitter are the obvious ones that a lot of people use. Maybe your own website, or other key community websites, will prove important as well.

- Then, below that, there are plenty of other social networks you might want to use to drive traffic, but bear in mind you have to master the top tier properly before you have time to do the second and third tiers. Don't post a single message on 50 websites, as that won't really help. You've got to be there building a community, engaging with people on a human level. Don't turn into a spam bot.

To empower your audience to promote your campaign, you can create a media pack supporters can use. This is a download with some nice images, maybe some social media avatars, and text summarising the project.

Suggest a campaign hashtag and use it as much as you can. Obviously, don't use it when you're talking about what you had for breakfast, but whenever it's relevant to the campaign, have the hashtag in there. This is a nice way of allowing people to feel included in the campaign.

When you're asking people to tweet, ask them to use the hashtag. Who knows, you might even be able to make it trend.

BUILDING YOUR SCHEDULE

It's critical you plan ahead and build a schedule at the very start. It's going to take a lot of time and energy to put this campaign together, and it's important you're not just reacting to events but working as part of a wider strategy. That means you're going to be prepared for what's to come and can feel there's light at the end of the tunnel when it's all getting too much. You'll be able to see that you're moving from one stage to another.

Generally, you want to spend at least as long in the pre-release phase as in the actual campaign. So, if you're going to do a 30-day campaign, you have to be spending at least 30 days really working on setting everything up. If you try and rush it, I think you'll lose out in the eventual campaign.

So let's have a look at how you might actually break down a typical 30-day crowdfunding campaign.

The first thing to notice in Figure 3.14 is that there are 14 weeks on this schedule. That's

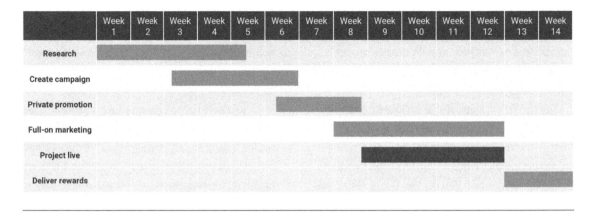

FIG 3.14 BREAKDOWN OF A TYPICAL 30-DAY CROWDFUNDING CAMPAIGN

over three months. So let's start with research: what's your topic, what's your subtopic, who are your audience, what's the best angle for your campaign, etc.?

You're also looking at how your audience speak to each other, and where they are connecting, so you can define them. Then you're looking at other creators who have run similar campaigns in the past, learning from the best and avoiding the things you see in the worst. I recommend you spend at least a month doing this, or as much as time will allow. After a couple of weeks, you'll have an idea what you should be doing. You'll realise there are patterns to the projects that were successful.

Research work isn't full-time; you can probably do it while working on other things. There's no need for you to quit your job at this stage. But as you start to build your campaign, the demands on your time are going to be greater.

As you get into the creation of your campaign, you'll start writing your pitch, scripting your video message and planning when and how you are going to shoot it, film it and edit it – making sure

it works. Once you have a clear idea what your campaign is and have drafted it, checked it for typos and got your video working, it's time for private promotion. This is where you talk to your friends and family, asking them for feedback. Maybe you'll start to reach out to some of the other groups as well; to some of the people who might be important gatekeepers for your audience.

A week or so before you're ready to launch the campaign, you are full-on marketing. By this point you'll have already worked out who you'll be contacting, so you're starting to say 'Hey, I've got this campaign coming out next week, can I count on your support, can you help me, or do you have any feedback for me?' You're still obviously open to feedback, and you might be using the technique of asking people for feedback in order to get them interested, but ultimately you know what your campaign is and are trying to politely get the word out.

Ultimately, when you come to launch your campaign, everything should be completely ready. You've got your team, you've got your pitch ready, you know your audience, you've already made links with all these people, and you're ready to hit the button. Some crowdfunding platforms require the campaign to be approved, so allow between two and three working days. Check which site you're going to use, what their process is and how long it's going to take. (Later in the book I'm going to discuss the Kickstarter process.)

Then you've got your actual 30-day campaign. It's full-on right from the moment you launch as a lot of the money is gathered during the first few days, as well as the last couple. Every single waking moment, you're contacting people, building connections, thanking backers, talking to your audience, updating the campaign, adding new rewards, and hopefully, when you get to the end of the 30 days, you've raised your money (you can sleep now).

But there is still work to be done. There are a lot of people to thank and rewards to send out. It's really important that you make time to thank everybody who helped you, even in a small way because:

- It's nice; it is human decency.

- You might need them again in the future if you're going to raise more money or if you're going to run another campaign.

- They might be eventual customers, people who promote the final version of your film.

So, keep a list as you go of all the people who've helped you and the people you owe thanks to. When it comes to this stage, write a more personal email to each one, with something that makes it unique to them, even if everything else is a little bit more generic. That way you can thank them in a meaningful way.

WHEN TO LAUNCH YOUR CAMPAIGN

If it's a 30-day campaign, you have to consider when you're launching and also when your deadline is. Most people are quite impatient to start their campaign, but bear in mind that you need to find the perfect time, and if that means waiting a month, or even two or three, wait. You can be using that extended deadline to improve your campaign to eventually reach more people.

Don't pick the date and time of launch purely according to when suits you. Look for relevant events or anniversaries.

Most of the money is raised in the first, second and last few days, so these are going to be critical.

Make sure you're also planning your own time, ensuring you're around to give the campaign the time it needs. You can't afford to be on holiday during the last few days of the campaign. (You can't afford to be on holiday at any point during the campaign, but least of all then!)

USE RELEVANT MAJOR EVENTS

Look for relevant upcoming events or anniversaries over the next few months that could increase the audience's interest. Press outlets are always on the lookout for unusual ways to cover stories and so you might be able to convince them to feature your project as a way of covering a particular related event or anniversary.

Sporting events might help you in the middle of your campaign if your campaign is about sport. You shouldn't expect to get a lot of donations at this point, but it will help keep the conversation alive. If you've got a rugby film, don't engineer the deadline to be during the World Cup, but running the campaign around the same sort of time is probably not a bad idea.

Avoid your campaign ending on a public holiday, when people are out of the house.

USE TOOLS LIKE GOOGLE TRENDS

Google Trends allows you to pick one or more search terms and see comparatively how interest in them changed over time. In Figure 3.15, I've put in 'Strictly Come Dancing', which is a television show, just to show you how it completely changes. The interest comes and goes based on when each season is on-air, as you can see over the years. I can tell you from this exactly when the series was launched and when the finale was. This might be useful for discovering historical trends, such as when

in the year, which parts of the month, or even which days are most useful for your topic.

CONSIDER YOUR AUDIENCE'S TIME ZONES

If you're making a Japanese thriller and are based in the UK, bear in mind a lot of your audience might be in Japan. Therefore, you don't want your launch or deadline times to be 3 a.m. in Tokyo. That last hour, just before you're closing, might push a lot of people to give you some money, and you can't afford to have them asleep.

PREDICTABLE CYCLES

Most people are paid at the end of every month. Depending on the make-up of your audience, this could have a huge or negligible effect – only you can judge.

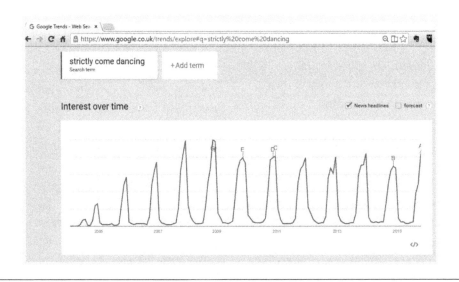

FIG 3.15 USING GOOGLE TRENDS TO PLAN YOUR CROWDFUNDING CAMPAIGN

SEASONAL FACTORS

People tend to have less money in December and January because of Christmas. However, if you can ensure a reward is shipped in time for Christmas, that can be very beneficial. The vast majority of DVDs in the UK are sold in November and December, and people are often looking for innovative and different gifts. Hopefully, you've got something innovative and different within your rewards. You could be offering it as a Christmas present, although the word of warning is to make sure you can ship it in time. It's one thing to ship rewards late and something else entirely to make people miss their Christmas deadlines – that's just not fair.

CONSIDERING THE DAY OF THE WEEK

Based on my research (shown in Figure 3.16), Tuesday is the most common day for new film projects and Sunday is the least popular.

Consider the environments your audience are most likely to be in when browsing your campaign – at home, in the office, etc. Then factor in how the days of the week will affect this. For example, if you're aiming the campaign at office workers, you don't want to be launching on a Saturday or Sunday.

Here's a nifty little trick: if you launch early on a Monday, you have the best shot at gaming the Kickstarter algorithm. Kickstarter haven't said this themselves, but a number of other sites have. Apparently, their 'what's hot' algorithm resets on Sunday night, so a quick spike on Monday morning could send you to the top, thereby gaining extra visibility and traffic. So, if you have a load of people to give you traffic when you launch, consider doing it early on a Monday.

CONSIDERING THE FINAL DAY

The final day of the campaign will be crucial for pushing your wavering supporters to donate. Therefore you want to ensure you've picked a day and time when they will be most reachable.

As the data presented in Figure 3.17 reveals, there is a small but significant negative effect of ending on a Sunday.

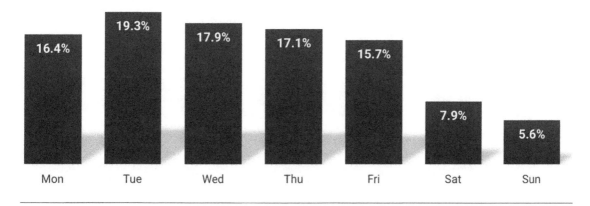

FIG 3.16 DAY OF THE WEEK PROJECTS ARE LAUNCHED

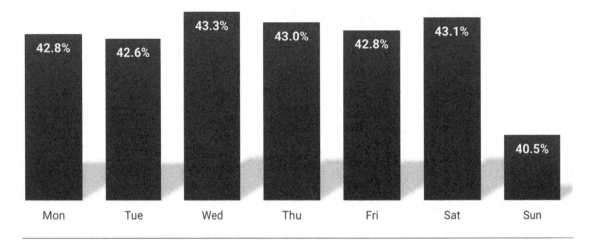

FIG 3.17 SUCCESS RATE BY FINAL DAY OF THE CAMPAIGN

YOUR TEAM

Let's talk about your team. It's very, very hard to run a successful crowdfunding campaign on your own. It is possible, but I don't think you really want to.

It can get a bit lonely, so you do need other people to support you. Also, the more people you have, the better ideas you're going to have on the table (in theory). And even if you actually can do it all, and you come up with the best ideas, you're going to have a problem with the amount of time you can spend on it. You'll need people to carry out the tasks you can't.

Every area of your campaign needs someone to love it – even the small details.

When you're working out what you're going to do yourself and which tasks to farm out, consider which of these three statements applies to each area (Figure 3.18):

1. **'I'm good at this'**, in which case you'd better be. Make sure you are up to date on this topic, and that you aren't afraid to take advice to improve.

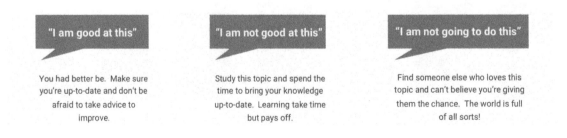

FIG 3.18 THREE STATEMENTS TO CONSIDER WHEN DECIDING WHICH TASKS TO PERFORM YOURSELF AND WHICH TO DELEGATE

2. **'I'm not good at this'**, but it's something you want to do, so you need to get better at it. Study the topic and spend the time to bring your knowledge up to date. Learning takes time, but it does pay off. In the months leading up to the campaign, you might want to develop new skills.

3. **'I'm not going to do this.'** If you're not going to do something, acknowledge it, even if you're just looking to palm off the things you think will be hard or boring. The world is a big place and somewhere there is a person who loves the idea of doing the stuff you hate.

THE TYPES OF PEOPLE YOU NEED IN YOUR TEAM

Let's look first at the people who are going to support you. Find some people who can help you brainstorm **creative ideas** for rewards, the headline and every other aspect of the campaign. These are people whom you can normally pay in thanks or just by taking them out for a meal while you talk it over.

Then you're going to need **experience**. This may exist in your current circle, but it's more likely that what you need to do is find similar campaigns to yours that have run in the past, and then reach out to those people: 'Hey, I saw you ran a campaign a year ago similar to the one I'm thinking of doing. Would you be around for a ten-minute Skype conversation?'

In my research, I've been approaching a lot of filmmakers who have made crowdfunding campaigns and almost every single one of them has been open to talking to me about it and very candid about what they've learned. They may join your team as mentors or they may give you a little piece of advice that will be useful in tweaking your campaign.

You're also going to need support from **your loved ones**. You might not need your significant other to sit there tweeting on your behalf, but they'll need to be prepared for you to be consumed by this campaign for a while. Let them know it's important to you and what's coming up.

Next, you need people to help with the creation and running of the campaign. I call

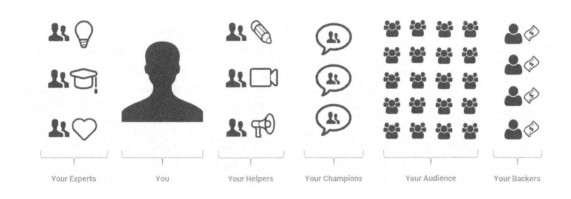

| Your Experts | You | Your Helpers | Your Champions | Your Audience | Your Backers |

FIG 3.19 THE TYPES OF PEOPLE YOU NEED IN YOUR CAMPAIGN TEAM

these people your **helpers**. This includes **writing the pitch** – they may write it entirely or just give you feedback on typos and things like that. You'll also need a team to help you **shoot the video**. You can shoot it yourself but, again, another set of people can help you make it to a higher standard.

And then you're going to need people who are going to shout on your behalf, the **marketing people**. These people will be emailing, tweeting, commenting and doing all manner of things to get the word out there about your campaign. They will help you amplify your voice and reach your **champions**.

The champions won't see themselves as being part of the campaign, but they will make a significant contribution by bringing it to a much larger and wider audience. Despite not officially being part of 'The Team', these people will need some coordination and instruction to ensure they're all on-message and up to date with developments.

These people will help you reach your **audience** – the people who are viewing your site, watching your videos and hopefully engaging through comments and conversations. Most will just observe, but a small number will convert into backers. The trick is that you don't know which ones will convert, so you need to engage with everyone.

So, as you can see, it's not a case of just you and the backers chatting – you need people behind you to support you and spread the word.

TIPS FOR BUILDING YOUR TEAM

Look around you and consider the strengths of the people who may be willing to help. What does each of them love doing? Passion is a vital part of crowdfunding, so ideally every member of your team won't be able to believe their luck when it comes to the tasks they've been set. People work much harder on something they love doing than something they've been forced or cajoled into.

Give people a chance to grow. If someone hasn't run a social media campaign before but has always been an assistant, they may be keen to work with you as you'll give them an opportunity to step up.

Define everyone's roles in advance. You don't have to give out titles like 'Head of Marketing' or 'Head of Outreach' if you don't want to, but it's important everyone knows what everyone else is doing and how it's connected to their work.

Make sure everybody on the team shares the same goal. You can't have some people thinking it's a comedy and some thinking it's a drama. You need everyone to have the same vision of what the eventual project will be, and the same vision of what the campaign is going to be. You really only get this by talking through your plans with the team in detail, so include them in as many parts as you can.

Get people who are involved with the final film to assist the funding campaign. You already know them, they have a vested interest in getting the funding, and if you've not worked with them before it's a good way to test the waters before moving on to the final film.

They're also great people to help spread the word because they don't just say 'Here is a campaign I think is great', they say 'Here is my campaign'. 'Join us' is an incredibly powerful statement; 'Join them' less so.

A word of warning: creatives are not natural sales people. Here are three tips to help you with that:

- **Help, support and encourage them to push harder.** They may feel they've tweeted all they can and emailed all the people they know, but they probably haven't. Talk to them about it and give them help to write these emails. Encourage them to go further than their natural comfort zone.

- **Give them the key talking points and some sales advice.** If you know a lot about sales, run your own little bootcamp for a couple of hours. If you don't, Google it and find the top ten selling tips for selling on the phone or by email and communicate that to your team.

- **If all else fails, find experienced sales people and bring them on to the team.** You can either incentivise them with money or sell them on the idea of it by saying 'Hey, come and join us, it's going to be fun and you'll get to do something different'. Even one experienced salesperson will have a transformative effect on the whole team.

CRAFTING YOUR **CAMPAIGN STORY**

At the heart of your pitch is going to be a single story. This is not the story contained in your final film; it's the story of you (and your team) as you take on the challenge of funding and making this film.

You need to find a single narrative to hang your entire campaign on. So what could it be? Look for the most interesting and compelling elements of the task ahead of you.

You're looking for things people want to hear about, not things you want to say. There's a big difference between the two so try and put yourself in the shoes of your target audience as they browse the net in a fit of boredom. What would pique their interest?

It could be:

- **The topic.** If it's quite broad it may not work, but if you pin it down to a unique subsection of a wider topic it might. Rather than saying it's about, say, planes, you could pin it down to a specific type of plane.

- **The genre.** If your film is a classic type of horror film that's not made much any more this could be the basis of your uniqueness.

- **The location.** If you're in a part of the world which doesn't get many film crews, this could be interesting. The opposite would be to run a campaign based on the idea that someone is finally making a film in LA! Not gonna work, right?

- **A famous cast or crew member.** This could be a celebrity or just an expert in their field. If you're making a film about a rocket ship, having a NASA engineer would be a fun element. Put them front and centre, answering questions, tweeting and sharing their knowledge.

- **How you're going to film it.** You might be using a unique shooting technique, such as doing it all in a single shot or all using drones. Have a quick Google before you commit to this as it could be that you're not the first and you've just not heard of the other projects that have already done this.

- **A topical element**, such as a large news or sporting event or a **significant anniversary** that's relevant to your campaign. There have been quite a few projects around the First World War recently to mark the 100-year anniversary of many of the key events.

- **The internet memes** which are popular online at the moment. Be careful you don't link your whole campaign to a passing fad, but if you can get it right, you can ride all of the existing support and goodwill around the meme.

- **Universal attractors**, such as things which are cute and funny. If this is your angle, make sure it's the cutest or funniest thing ever; the internet is awash with such things and you need to be in the top tier to get noticed.

This list is not exhaustive, of course; the hook can be anything interesting or compelling. When you find the element you're going to build your campaign around, make sure it's really simple, really clear and echoed in everything you put out.

Remember that this is the angle of your campaign, not the final film. I'm not suggesting you change your final film to bend to the crowdfunding audience. That said, make sure there's a strong link between the campaign and the film or you could leave your backers feeling tricked when it's finally released.

People want to live vicariously through you so you need to give them a passionate story to believe in. Don't tell them 'We're going to make a film, it's small but it's okay'. Tell them 'It's going to be amazing. There is a chance it may not work, it's a risk, but come on in and join us on the journey'.

STORY ARCS FOR YOUR CAMPAIGN PITCH

If you're telling people a story about your journey, you should pick a story arc that inspires people to take action. There are many types of

The Challenge Plot

Against all the odds the little hero stands up to the massive giant

The Connection Plot

Bridging seemingly-insurmountable differences or barriers to connect

The Creativity Plot

Smart, creative or ingenious use of the everyday environment

FIG 4.1 STORY ARCS FOR YOUR CAMPAIGN PITCH

story in the world but three in particular can do this (see Figure 4.1).

- **The challenge plot.** Against all odds, the little hero stands up to an opponent much bigger and stronger than they are. In many cases it doesn't matter if they succeed or not; what matters is that they've chosen to stand up. This inspires people to take action in their own lives. Apparently this is more effective with men than women.

- **The connection plot.** Despite huge obstacles, two beings are able to connect. Think *Romeo & Juliet* or *Titanic*. It could be romance or just unlikely people coming together, such as in *The Shawshank Redemption*. Apparently this is most effective with women.

- **The creativity plot.** An example of a story with a creativity plot is *MacGyver*, in which the titular character would find creative and ingenious uses for everyday objects. Watching these types of stories inspires us to make creative changes in our own lives. This works equally well on men and women.

THE FIVE REASONS PEOPLE SHARE THINGS ONLINE

- **Practical value** – Tap into your audience's inner caveman

- **Social currency** – Make people look good when they share

- **Triggers** – Tap into familiar items to trigger associations

- **Public** – Being seen to share, and feeling included

- **Emotion** – When we care, we share

WHAT TO INCLUDE IN YOUR PITCH

Let's look at the main concept behind your whole crowdfunding campaign – what I'm calling The Pitch.

Everything you do, be it text, images, videos, conversations or marketing should echo this central idea.

	High Arousal	Low Arousal
Positive	Awe Excitement Amusement	Contentment
Negative	Anger Anxiety	Sadness

FIG 4.2 HOW AUDIENCES REACT TO DIFFERENT EMOTIONS

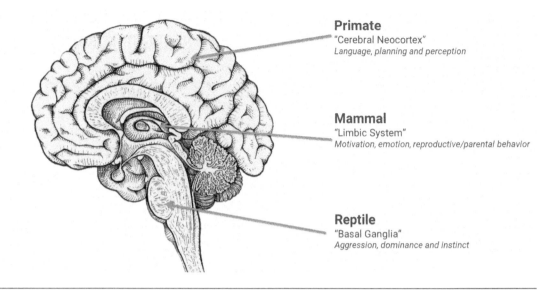

Primate
"Cerebral Neocortex"
Language, planning and perception

Mammal
"Limbic System"
Motivation, emotion, reproductive/parental behavior

Reptile
"Basal Ganglia"
Aggression, dominance and instinct

FIG 4.3 THE FUNCTIONS OF DIFFERENT PARTS OF THE BRAIN

Earlier we looked at the three types of story that motivate the most amount of action: the challenge plot, the connection plot and the creativity plot. Find the one of these which best fits your narrative and shape your messaging around that.

On the crowdfunding page you want lots for the audience to view, read and interact with. This will reward their time and loyalty.

First of all you need text explaining what you do, who you are and why it matters for you to be funded.

You'll need imagery and a video – we'll look at these in detail later on.

You should introduce your team, set your timeframe, explain your goal and detail how you will spend the money.

To establish some frequently asked questions, ask everyone you show the campaign to in its early stages if they have queries. Never dismiss a question as being stupid. It might seem stupid to you, but whether it is or not, many people might have the same question, so it's important to address it in the FAQs.

Finally you need to end by being clear about the risks and challenges.

Let's go through each of these elements.

THE HEADLINE

Start with the angle you defined at the beginning of this chapter. This is the element in your campaign that you think is fresh, different, interesting and will relate to your core audience.

Write this down as simply as possible on a Post-it and stick it on your monitor. Honestly, it will help you focus on it.

Figure 4.4 gives an example. 'Our story is that no one has ever shot a feature film in our town before, which is crazy because it has the best people and the most interesting stories.'

This is the central theme for the campaign and so everything created for the campaign will come from this idea. Why has no one shot there before? Did anyone come close to it? What's the town like? What are the people like?

From that, you need to craft your first public element: **the headline**.

A bad example would be 'My Town'. It might be a valid name for the final film but it doesn't convey enough to work for the crowdfunding campaign. The worst reaction you can get to any element of your campaign is 'So what?' – and that's what this headline might get.

A couple of better examples would be 'My town... a comedy feature film where no one has shot before' or 'My town, the first feature film made in my town'.

You don't have an endless amount of space. Kickstarter allows a maximum of 61 characters and Indiegogo 50.

Road-test the options by showing them to friends and asking them what they would expect from a campaign with this name. If this doesn't match what's on your Post-it note, you need to go back to the drawing board.

FIG 4.4 YOUR CAMPAIGN NEEDS A CENTRAL THEME, OR ANGLE

THE SUBTITLE

There should also be a short blurb or subtitle – the text that goes underneath your title and sums up your campaign.

A bad example of this would be 'I want to make a feature because I think it will be fun'. You've centred it on yourself, which means anybody else will probably just think 'Well, so what? I don't care about that'.

A more interesting line to engage the audience would be 'We have an incredibly funny script, an awesome team and a location you've never seen before on screen. Help us make this town's first ever feature film'. This is more interesting and engaging, and uses tangible, vivid language. It's really giving you something different and is inviting you in.

Another example might be 'We want to make the town's first ever feature film, but we will need your help, love, support, cash and socks. It's in our town. It's cold here'. This is far more personal and may or may not suit your style, but it gives people a flavour straight away of who you are and what your campaign is about.

Kickstarter blurbs are limited to 135 characters and at Indiegogo it's 100.

THE MAIN DESCRIPTION

Below this you will have your main text description.

Kickstarter's maximum description is 35,000 characters so you have a lot of space to use. To give you a sense of scale, if you open up a new Word document and start typing, you'll hit 35,000 characters about halfway down the ninth page (Calibri font, size 11).

Kickstarter says you can write your description in any language, but they do recommend an English translation. A lot of the audience going to Kickstarter is in America and therefore speak mostly English.

Here are my tips for crafting your description:

1. **Take your time in drafting and redrafting it.** This is a pivotal part of your campaign and needs to be the best it can be.

2. **Don't skimp on the detail.** Looking at the chart in Figure 4.5 we can spot two patterns. First, campaign descriptions are getting longer. This is a consequence of both the increasingly professional nature of crowdfunding campaigns and the fact that audiences demand more detail from campaign creators.

    Second, successful campaigns tend to have longer descriptions than those campaigns that failed. Obviously, writing more just for the sake of it won't magically make your campaign more likely to reach its goal. But a well-written description that addresses everything the audience wants to know is likely to be much longer than a lazily written one.

3. **Make it conversational, but professional.** Every project and every person will have their own 'tone of voice'; you need to find a happy medium between too conversational and too corporate. You don't want it to sound like you're a bunch of guys who have no idea how you're going to achieve the project, but you also want to avoid sounding like a boring PR agency, or a corporation that has no soul. You want to sound like real people who have put the effort in to make the project look and sound good.

4. **Keep it on message.** Don't get drawn into writing your whole life story. There should be a strong connection with video, the rewards and the overall story, with all

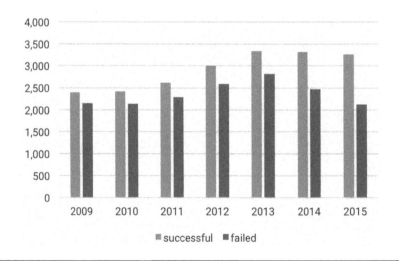

FIG 4.5 AVERAGE NUMBER OF CHARACTERS IN THE CAMPAIGN DESCRIPTION FOR KICKSTARTER FILM PROJECTS

elements telling different sides of the same story. The best way to do this is by keeping focused on that Post-it on your monitor.

TIPS FOR WRITING YOUR PITCH

AVOID BUZZWORDS AND INDUSTRY TERMS

Don't use words or terminology your wider audience won't understand. You might have to reach a whole new audience to meet your target goal and they'll be put off by words they don't understand.

APPEAL TO PEOPLE'S EMOTIONS

Use words like 'join', 'support', 'participate', rather than 'help', 'need', 'money'. Try to make people support you.

FOCUS ON IT FROM THE AUDIENCE'S POINT OF VIEW

What are the benefits for the backers? Not the benefits for you. The benefits for you are pretty obvious: you get money, you get to make a film. You want to make a film, and that's wonderful. But what will the people who support you get out of it?

EMPHASISE THAT THERE'S A LIMITED TIME PERIOD

This is the case all the way through the campaign, but especially so towards the end. Be sure to let people know that 'It's now or never, guys, so come on! We need the support, it makes all the difference'.

ASK INTELLIGENT QUESTIONS OF THE READER

You want your audience to mentally and emotionally engage with your campaign, so give them entry points to do so. Ask 'Why do you think no one has shot in our town before?' Don't treat them like four-year-olds; they're adults.

READ THE DESCRIPTIONS ON OTHER CAMPAIGNS

I've read a huge number of campaigns for my research and the same things tend to crop up over and over again. You start seeing what works and what doesn't, based on how many times a particular strategy is used.

You should do this, too – find projects similar to yours and read them (they're all archived). You'll probably find a couple of campaigns out there that closed years ago that you really wish you could give money to, because you really like what they're doing. Then there will be others where you're part of the audience because of your hobbies, only they're not written in a way that's interesting to you.

SEEK FEEDBACK

Get feedback and take it onboard. When people are telling you the same thing, maybe they can see something you can't.

PROOFREAD. REPEAT.

Proofread again and again. I'm terrible with this; I'm dyslexic so I often get these things wrong. But I also find, when I read something that hasn't been prepared properly, that I assume

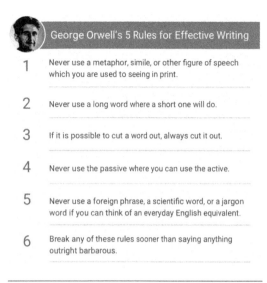

FIG 4.6

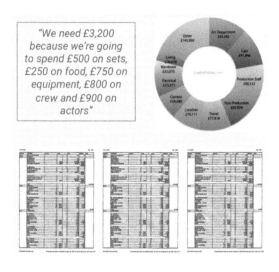

FIG 4.7 USE A CHART TO DISPLAY YOUR FILM'S BUDGET

not enough effort has gone into it. If you're asking for people's money and attention, the least you can do is make sure you ask them in an intelligent way.

LEARN FROM THE BEST

Figure 4.6 shows some useful tips by George Orwell on how to write effective copy.

EXPLAINING YOUR GOAL AMOUNT

In your pitch, you're going to have to explain the goal amount and why you need that much. This is an important part of making your audience trust you and feel like you know how to complete the film you're fundraising for.

SHOW IT VISUALLY

Your audience does not want a complete line-by-line Excel spreadsheet of your film's budget,

but they do expect to be able to glance at the topline budget and see that you know how you're going to spend the money if the campaign is successful. (If you do give the full detail, make sure you have a summary as well since most people won't want to read it.) If you can, show it visually in a chart (e.g. Figure 4.7) or at the very least an attractive table.

MAKE SURE IT MATCHES THE PROJECT AND TARGET GOAL

Kickstarter checks if your goal matches your stated budget, so don't get these things wrong. If you ask for £10,000 but can only account for £9,000, it's unlikely you'll be cleared for launch.

If you have a few items you feel will look bad to the audience, you could consider including them in an 'Other' category. That said, it's often best to be as open and honest with your audience as possible. Explain yourself fully and trust in their ability to understand your process. Whatever you do, don't lie to them.

BUILDING TRUST

The purpose of your campaign is to create trust between you and your audience and there are a number of ways you can do this:

1. **Always act in a professional manner.** This covers everything from tone of voice and making sure your figures add up to proof-reading all your work and generally acting like a professional.

2. **Be real and be visible.** Link to previous work by members of the team, and to their online accounts, such as credits on IMDb. Including links to their Facebook or Twitter accounts will act as proof that you're real, willing to be approached and not afraid to put your real name behind the campaign. Campaigns that only use a generic company name and don't link to previous projects are unlikely to engender trust in the audience.

3. **Invite people to get in contact.** Most crowd-funding platforms allow users to send direct messages to campaign creators. You should invite people to contact you and be sure to reply to every message. If you're getting a lot of messages, assign one or two members of your team to be in charge of answering. The vast majority of messages can be answered quickly, with only the complicated or important ones being elevated up the chain to you.

4. **Include recommendations and testimonials from respected or credible people.** If you have reviews of your previous films, include them, doubly so if they're from the *New York Times*. But, at the very least, they could be from audience members at a screening of one of your previous films. That enthusiasm could be infectious. Include press coverage as it happens. You can update your campaign, which means that, as each day goes by, your campaign becomes more trustworthy.

Figure 4.8 lays out a number of things that create and destroy trust.

Things that create trust are:

- **Detailed plans and explanations.** Say what you want to do and how you'll achieve it.

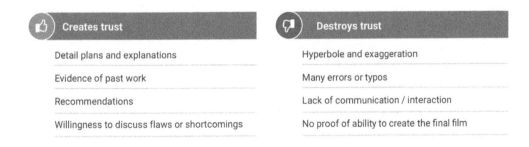

👍 Creates trust	👎 Destroys trust
Detail plans and explanations	Hyperbole and exaggeration
Evidence of past work	Many errors or typos
Recommendations	Lack of communication / interaction
Willingness to discuss flaws or shortcomings	No proof of ability to create the final film

FIG 4.8 THINGS THAT CREATE AND DESTROY TRUST

- **Evidence of past work.** This means they know you're not new on the scene and can see you've delivered in the past.

- **Recommendations from other humans and companies.** These can go quite far.

- **A willingness to discuss flaws or shortcomings.** Don't delete comments you don't like and don't ignore people when they raise a good point. If you take these onboard, it will only make your project stronger.

Things that can destroy trust are:

- **Hyperbole and exaggeration.** Don't exaggerate in a million, billion years.

- **Having many errors or typos.** Many people will forgive one or two but lots of them will make you lose trust.

- **A lack of communication and/or interaction.** There is no end of stories of people running a website or social media group online; then something bad happens and they disappear and delete their accounts. Nothing makes you look more guilty and untrustworthy than when you disappear. Even when the worst happens, talk to people.

- **Lack of proof of your ability to create the final film.** If you say you need $3 million to make the biggest 3D film ever, but you've never shot anything before and you can't put together an interesting, engaging normal video... well, no one is going to believe you can do this.

RISKS AND CHALLENGES

The final section, at the bottom of your campaign page, addresses the risks and challenges. This is where you manage expectations, own up, and discuss the things that can go wrong.

WRITE MORE RATHER THAN LESS

You don't want to be raising money under false pretences and you really don't want your backers to feel tricked or misled. Therefore, explain all of the things you think could go wrong and what steps you're taking to mitigate them. Don't just say 'terms and conditions apply'.

SOUND LIKE A HUMAN BEING

This section doesn't have to sound like the type of nasty small print we expect from banks. Instead, see it as a chance to level with your audience and be open about the challenges you'll face.

Here is a great example from Zach Braff from his *Wish I Was Here* campaign, which raised $3 million. He said:

> 'To sum it up, movie making is a crazy business, with a lot of unknown factors. We start with a script I'm really proud of. Then, we assemble the best team possible, get insurance, and make contingency plans. It's impossible to guarantee everything will come together exactly as planned, but in the end, we will have created a movie that hopefully all of us can be proud of. It's a great journey, and I thank you in advance if you can help make this ride possible.'

That campaign was a few years ago; I think today people would want a few more of the risks and challenges detailed. But what is undeniable is his human honesty.

EXAMPLES

Each project will have its own unique challenges, but here are a few examples of things you might want to consider:

- One of the key members of the team has to pull out.

- Environmental factors interfere with filming.

- The story evolves on-set or in the edit. They say you make a film three times: once when you write it down, once when you film it, and once when you edit it. This is universal to all film projects but if your film involves a lot of improvisation and you've set out the story in detail it may be worth mentioning especially.

- There are changes to the price or availability of kit or crew.

- New opportunities arise, meaning you need to change the plan. For example, a number of successful films have been offered distribution deals, which means backers can't be sent their DVDs on time.

- You can't guarantee the film will get mainstream distribution (unless you're physically doing it yourself).

- For trips to the set, you can't be sure where or when these will take place.

- To become an extra or crew member may require a visa or work permit.

IMAGERY

Crowdfunding campaigns for films need to be visually interesting, both because you need to attract people's attention and because you need to convince them you can make a beautiful film.

Be bold, be creative, be brave, but never, ever be boring with your images. Remember they should all match your overall pitch and the audience you're heading towards.

kickstarter.com/projects/removedfeature/removed-feature-film, kickstarter.com/projects/eoberts/fish-tank-a-short-film-by-ethan-Roberts, kickstarter.com/projects/2096262497/you-are-free-a-short-film, kickstarter.com/projects/peterplan/peter-plan-a-short-film-with-a-big-idea, kickstarter.com/projects/ParadigmaProductions/nothing-against-life-an-independent-feature-film-a, kickstarter.com/projects/jasmerrin/sleepwalkers-feature-film, kickstarter.com/projects/runicfilms/hashtag-short-film, kickstarter.com/projects/structurefilms/the-bill-nye-film, kickstarter.com/projects/dtum/seeking-asian-female/description, kickstarter.com/projects/1302553666/i-filmed-your-death-feature-film

FIG 4.9 EXAMPLES OF HERO IMAGES

I'm going to cover some of the key types of imagery you're probably going to need to create for your campaign, using examples from real crowdfunding film projects.

THE HERO IMAGE

This is the main image at the top of your campaign and is where people will pick up so much about your project. Looking at the examples in Figure 4.9 you'll see they're all very different and that each allows you to guess the genre of the film they represent. You want to be shouting your genre from the rooftops – your audiences need to be able to glance at your main image and just 'get' the essence of your campaign.

Don't try to pack too much into one image as simplicity often delivers a powerful message. In addition, if you cover your image in small text you could lose the overall message.

Take a moment to check out the size, ratio and acceptable formats of your chosen platform (see Figure 4.10 for Kickstarter and Indiegogo). Make sure your image isn't too small, otherwise it will look pixelated.

Note: Indiegogo used to allow animated GIFs but they removed this functionality in August 2015. So, if you see a GIF in an old campaign, this will be why.

You can update this image during the actual campaign, so this is a perfect way of letting your audience know how it's going. I wouldn't suggest you update it every day (e.g. 'We're 63% funded!') but you should certainly use it for the final few days or when new rewards are added.

LOGO

You might choose to create a brand around your film, including getting a logo designed. If you do, make sure you have it in all the different versions/sizes; ensure it can be used as a large hero image or small social media icon.

It might be as simple as just some text in a nice font, or it might be that you get something properly illustrated or even animated (Figure 4.11 shows some examples). This can add to the professional look of your campaign, but try not to get lost down the rabbit hole of spending weeks on it, at the expense of the rest of the campaign.

POSTER

A poster can make your film feel more 'alive' and can also be used as the DVD cover in your

K Kickstarter	GO Indiegogo
At least 1024 x 768 (4:3 ratio)	Recommended 640 x 640 (1:1 radio)
JPEG, PNG, GIF or BMP	At least 220 x 220
50mb limit	JPEG or PNG

FIG 4.10 ACCEPTABLE SIZE, RATIO AND FORMAT OF YOUR MAIN CAMPAIGN IMAGE WHEN USING KICKSTARTER AND INDIEGOGO

kickstarter.com/projects/515070734/made-men-the-film

kickstarter.com/projects/iluzijastudio/the-phantom-of-
the-opera-animated-stage-ii-script

FIG 4.11 EXAMPLES OF LOGOS

kickstarter.com/projects/evanviera/caldera-animated-
short-film

kickstarter.com/projects/878562580/youre-so-cool-
brewster-the-story-of-fright-night-d

FIG 4.12 EXAMPLES OF POSTER IMAGES

mock-ups. It's about conveying key information and setting the tone. The examples in Figure 4.12 make it easy to guess the tone and target audience.

Before you start working on it, perform some basic research on movie posters in your genre via IMDb, Amazon and Google. They may not always be works of art, but you'll see the techniques they use to convey subtle messages to the audience. For example, melancholic dramas often focus on the faces of their key cast, with no character looking at any other. Or take gross-out teen comedies, which often use white backgrounds and red text. You should mainly focus on posters from the same genre as your film.

Moviegoers have become very attuned to the semiotics of movie advertising, so this is a good chance for you to convey more about your film to the audience. It also gives people confidence that you know how to make this film well.

kickstarter.com/projects/johnclyons/unearth-a-feature-length-horror-film

kickstarter.com/projects/jasmerrin/sleepwalkers-feature-film/description

FIG 4.13 EXAMPLES OF PRODUCTION STILLS

PRODUCTION STILLS

Although you may not have shot your film yet, the audience is going to want to get a sense of what it will look like. Therefore you may want to take your key cast to locations similar to those in your script and shoot a few mock production stills, or even start filming part of the final film before the campaign begins.

Choose the most pivotal and visually interesting scenes and, within those scenes, find the best moment in time to concentrate on.

If your final film will have a distinctive look, ensure you grade these images to match. For reference, take a look at the images the press run for Hollywood movies as they tend to convey a large amount of information about the film in each one.

Creating the 'perfect' production still is harder than you think, so take the time to plan, take lots of shots on the day and test the images on a willing audience before deciding on the final choices. Rather than asking your test subjects 'Do you like this image?' ask them instead 'What is this scene/film about?' If they can't tell you something true to your film, the image is not one you should use.

ILLUSTRATE YOUR PITCH

There's a lot of information you'll want to convey in your main campaign description so images can be a good way to break up the text and make the campaign look more appealing. A prime candidate for this treatment is your budget as you can quickly let your audience know what the major costs categories are.

Be creative and try something innovative. For example, if your film stars a six-year-old character, have six-year-old children holding up big pieces of card detailing how much each element will cost.

If you're communicating data, the two major requirements are to make it easy to understand and enjoyable to look at.

kickstarter.com/projects/1221950308/float-short-film

kickstarter.com/projects/308634931 /the-staying-kind-a-short-film

FIG 4.14 EXAMPLES OF MOOD BOARDS

kickstarter.com/projects/572521277/ambitions-debt

kickstarter.com/projects/518273025/here-alone-a- feature-film-in-progress

FIG 4.15 EXAMPLES OF IMAGES OF CAST AND CREW

MOOD BOARD

If your film will have a distinctive or visually interesting look, you might consider including a mood board from the director. These are images you might have shot beforehand or found online that show what your film is going to look like.

They should come together to create one cohesive vision for the film, achieved by picking good images and grading them to match the director's vision.

Be mindful of copyright – you don't want to be basing your campaign on stolen images.

THE TEAM

You want to make people feel connected emotionally to your team, so definitely include pictures of the key cast and crew. If you can, also use them to give a sense of what the project is like – is it glossy and slick, or artistic and rough?

Figure 4.15 shows some examples, the one on the right being particularly beautiful, a hybrid between a photo and a painting. The URL is included in the figure in case you want to have a look at it.

CARTOONS

If it's appropriate, you might want to include cartoons. These could be sketches to illustrate how you feel the film will come across, or they could be something humorous to entertain and delight your audience. The one on the right of Figure 4.16 is from Pen Jillet's campaign where he raised $1.1 million.

STORYBOARDS

Storyboards help people visualise the final film. You might already have created many storyboards and it might be very easy for you to create more, but don't rely too much on them. They're attempting to show what the final film will look like, but may not add much to the pitch of your campaign. Your backers are less likely to be supporting your final film than your journey in trying to get it funded and made. So, you could

kickstarter.com/projects/elliottgonzo/yeast-short-film

fundanything.com/en/campaigns/penn-campaign

FIG 4.16 EXAMPLES OF CARTOONS USED TO ILLUSTRATE CROWDFUNDING PITCHES

kickstarter.com/projects/1221950308/float-short-film

kickstarter.com/projects/802290150/the-emperors-banquet

FIG 4.17 EXAMPLES OF CARTOONS USED TO ILLUSTRATE CROWDFUNDING PITCHES

kickstarter.com/projects/webeharebrained/battletech

kickstarter.com/projects/309114309/infinity-battlescape

FIG 4.18 EXAMPLES OF IMAGES USED IN CROWDFUNDING CAMPAIGNS

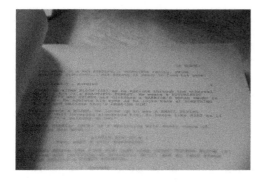

kickstarter.com/projects/1869987317/wish-i-was-here-1

kickstarter.com/projects/455421787/buzkashi-boys

FIG 4.19 EXAMPLES OF IMAGES USED IN CROWDFUNDING CAMPAIGNS

include a fun update video of you drawing the storyboards and really agonising over them, which might be more useful than the actual boards.

ARTWORK

You might be able to illustrate what your film is going to look like through some concept art. Concept art is usually very detailed and beautiful; it's not a storyboard. It gives your audience a sense of what things are going to look like and is especially relevant when you're creating new worlds, science fiction or alien planets – things we can't necessarily imagine for ourselves.

SELL THE SIZZLE

Remember you're making a movie and that movies are really cool and fun, so you'll want to sell the 'sizzle', the exciting stuff. So, photos of cameras, scripts, clapperboards, etc. could excite a non-filmmaking audience.

Obviously this might not work on an audience of film professionals, but, as with all these images,

kickstarter.com/projects/elliottgonzo/yeast-short-film

kickstarter.com/projects/sfgreenfilmfest/4th-annual-san-francisco-green-film-festival

FIG 4.20 IMAGES OF SAMPLE REWARDS ON OFFER FOR SUPPORTING THE CAMPAIGN

you need to judge what's most appropriate and tailor them to who will be looking at your campaign.

SHOW THE REWARDS

Finally, visualise the rewards. Show people what they're going to get. If it's a product, make sure you give a very clear idea of how it will look. If it's an experience, let people feel part of something. In Figure 4.20, the image on the right is from San Francisco Green Film Festival. You really get a sense that there are going to be events with nice people interacting. It feels welcoming. So, if that was the illustration for buying a ticket, it would be far better than just a picture of a ticket.

THE **REWARDS**

BUILDING YOUR REWARDS

Let's turn to the rewards you're going to offer. Remember, on Indiegogo they're called 'perks', but as most crowdfunding platforms call them rewards that's the word I'm going to use here.

Most sites require you to offer something in return for contributions, although the backers are allowed to refuse the reward (making it a pure donation) and what you offer them can be as simple as a thank you in the credits of the film or online.

When you're building your rewards, think about what's going to delight and surprise your audience. Brainstorming rewards should take time because you want to throw out the obvious and the boring. I suggest involving some of your team and making a game of who can come up with the best ones. Write down all ideas, even the ones you don't like, as you never know how far away a dumb idea is from a genius one – sometimes it just takes a bit of time to realise it.

Go through other crowdfunding campaigns and jot down the rewards you like. Again, this could be a competition among the team to find the best ones from other campaigns.

Part of the reason for making it a team effort is that the perfect reward is one you can't wait to tell other people about. This is part of what will motivate your audience to share your campaign online.

Each reward should have a target audience and a clear benefit to those people.

If you're aiming to reach multiple audience groups with the campaign, you need rewards to appeal to all people on all budgets.

The perfect reward from your point of view is non-physical, meaning it should be easy to deliver, and allows you to create more rewards without increased manufacturing costs.

Make some of the rewards finite in number and tell your audience that once they're gone, they're gone. Scarcity motivates more than an unlimited supply.

🇺🇸	United States	USD $10,000
🇬🇧	United Kingdom	GBP £5,000
🇨🇦	Canada	CAD $8,000
🇦🇺	Australia	AUD $8,000
🇳🇿	New Zealand	NZD $8,000
🇸🇪	Sweden	SEK 50,000
🇩🇰	Denmark	DKK 50,000
🇳🇴	Norway	NOK 50,000
🇨🇭	Switzerland	CHF 7,000
	Netherlands, Germany, Italy, Austria, Spain, Luxembourg, France, Belgium and Ireland	EUR €7,000

FIG 5.1 MAXIMUM SIZES OF INDIVIDUAL REWARDS ON KICKSTARTER

Bear in mind that preparing and shipping your rewards will take longer than you think. You need to state a rough timeframe for when the backers can expect to receive them and it's best to give yourself a bit of extra time.

REWARD SIZES

Indiegogo doesn't currently have a maximum reward size but Kickstarter does.

The maximum single reward you can offer on a US-based campaign is $10,000. Obviously, you can create infinite numbers of them, but you can't give $50,000 in a single reward. Figure 5.1 shows the maximum rewards for projects in various other countries.

Because of currency conversions this means US projects can offer the largest rewards. Projects based in New Zealand are limited to the equivalent of about $5,400.

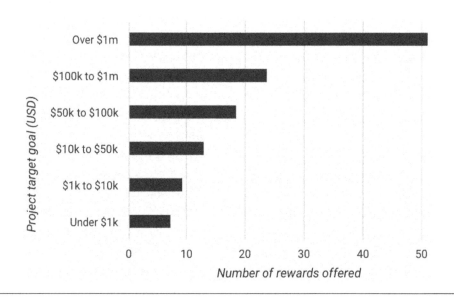

FIG 5.2 AVERAGE NUMBER OF REWARDS ON KICKSTARTER FILM PROJECTS

HOW MANY REWARDS SHOULD YOU OFFER?

First of all, don't just create a huge number. With too many you won't be able to make a clear pitch to your backers and the best ones could get lost in the crowd. However, if you have too few, you could end up missing out on money from backers as they couldn't find anything they wanted.

You need to offer rewards to each audience group, and within that have a tier system. So, for example, you could have $5, $25, $100 and $500 – for each audience group.

Figure 5.2 shows the number of rewards film projects on Kickstarter have offered in the past.

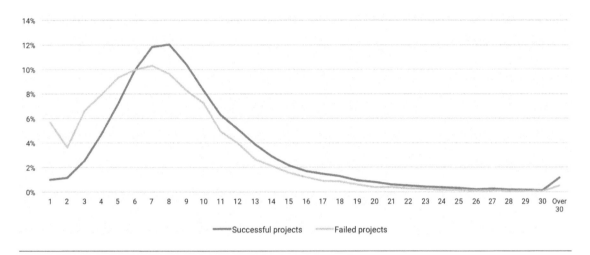

FIG 5.3 KICKSTARTER PROJECTS THAT FAILED AGAINST THOSE THAT SUCCEEDED

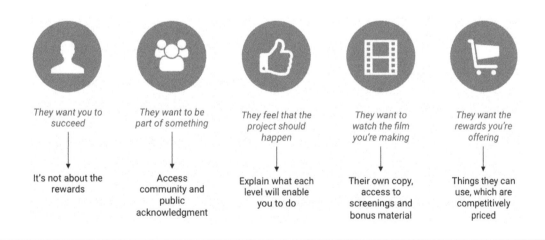

They want you to succeed	They want to be part of something	They feel that the project should happen	They want to watch the film you're making	They want the rewards you're offering
It's not about the rewards	Access community and public acknowledgment	Explain what each level will enable you to do	Their own copy, access to screenings and bonus material	Things they can use, which are competitively priced

FIG 5.4 REASONS WHY PEOPLE DONATE TO CROWDFUNDING CAMPAIGNS

The smallest projects offer only a handful whereas the really big ones offer over 50 on average.

In Figure 5.3 I've split the findings into successfully funded projects and those which failed. As you can see, the successful projects offered slightly more rewards, but not by a massive amount. Successful Kickstarter film projects have an average of ten rewards and unsuccessful campaigns have an average of eight.

Indiegogo says 70% of successful projects offer between three and eight rewards tiers.

There is a correlation between success rate and number of rewards offered. The higher the number of rewards, the higher the success rate. We shouldn't read this to mean 'I should offer a million rewards as then I'm guaranteed to succeed!' but instead that if you offer people too few rewards, you may be turning backers away.

WHY PEOPLE GIVE TO CROWDFUNDING CAMPAIGNS

We've already seen, in Figure 3.4, the main reasons people give to crowdfunding campaigns. Let's go through these again in the specific context of rewards:

- **They want you to succeed.** These people don't really need rewards. They want acknowledgement and personal thanks. Your auntie doesn't want a T-shirt – she wants a phone call.

- **They want to be part of something.** They want to join you on the journey, so carve out a place for them to have exclusive updates and access. They may appreciate credit on the film more than most, as well as a tweet or public thanks. You could also make very limited edition rewards which are only open to early bird backers or the first 25 people to claim them.

- **They feel the project should happen.** Create rewards which are related to the impact their donation will have on the project. So, if a $500 reward allows you to shoot it in 3D, say you'll make a 3D poster just for them – you'll probably need to offer more as well, but this part highlights the benefit of their contribution.

- **They want to watch the film you're making.** The standard filmmaker reward is a DVD but, as we get more used to Video on Demand, more people are going to want to be able to watch it online. On the low end that's great as it's much cheaper to give someone a password or login than to send them a physical disc. However, it leaves you with a problem on the higher ends. If you can't create a special edition double disc box set, how can you justify a $100 reward to these types of people? You could create earlier access or access to rough cuts (although check with your director first as they may not be so keen on that!).

- **They want the rewards you're offering.** For these people you are simply a shop, so make sure you're creating rewards that can compete with Amazon.com products. You can't compete on price (because they have scale and also because you need to make a much higher profit margin), so you're going to have to go for special, different or unique. Find products that are selling well and put a new spin on them.

Thank you   Tweet   Credit on the film   The script   More content

FIG 5.5 EXAMPLES OF $1 REWARDS

$1 REWARDS

During my research I started to notice a fair number of campaigns offering a $1 reward level. I dug deeper and discovered that 27% of Kickstarter film projects have $1 rewards. This intrigued me, as this tiny amount of money is clearly neither here nor there when it comes to achieving your campaign's goal.

So, what can be achieved with a $1 reward? Quite a lot of things, it turns out.

A $1 reward increases the number of people who are feeling emotionally invested in your campaign.

It also gives you a way to communicate with them more often and in a much more personal way than simply via public updates. This means you can try and turn them into larger backers or, at the very least, get additional social sharing from them.

It also acts as social proof that your campaign is popular and can gain an audience. This in turn will lead to more people becoming backers and more shares.

There's a guy on eBay who sells guitar strings for $1, which is kind of crazy because guitar strings should cost a lot more. He's selling them at a loss and has been doing so for a number of

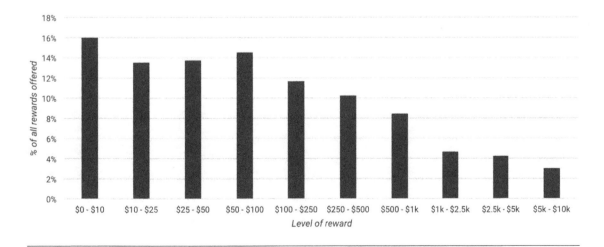

FIG 5.6 KICKSTARTER REWARD LEVELS OFFERED

years. Why is he doing this? Well, he also sells guitars, and by losing a tiny bit of money on the strings he gets the contact details of guitar fans who already know and like his company. Very smart move.

There are a number of things you can offer in return for $1. You want to be careful not to offer things people might be happy to pay more for. Here are a few examples:

- A public thank you

- A tweet or a follow

- A 'With thanks' credit on the film

- A PDF copy of the script

- Access to your behind-the-scenes website, which would be more about building an audience and upselling to them later, as with the guitar strings

From my research shown in Figure 5.6 you can see that, for Kickstarter, most reward levels offered are under $100. Indiegogo say their most commonly claimed reward is $25.

BUDGETING YOUR REWARDS

Once you have some ideas for your rewards you'll want to cost them out to make sure they're financially viable.

Here's a simple calculation you should perform for each reward:

- The price of the reward

- Minus the 5% platform fee and 3% processing fee (if you're using Kickstarter or Indiegogo)

£20 reward
Get a signed
DVD

−£1.80
5% fee
3% + £0.20 processing

−£2.50
Creating the
DVD

−£2.26
Envelope and
postage to UK

You receive
£13.44

FIG 5.7 BUDGETING YOUR REWARDS

£20 reward
Get a signed
DVD

−£5.80
5% fee
3% + £0.20 processing
20% VAT

−£2.50
Creating the
DVD

−£2.26
Envelope and
postage to UK

You receive
£9.44

FIG 5.8 CALCULATING YOUR PROFIT AFTER CHARGES

- Minus the physical cost of creation, including adaptation if you're signing it or changing it in any way

- Minus the cost of packing and shipping

So let's work through an example (Figure 5.7).

If you've got a £20 DVD reward, deducting the fees, cost of creation and postage leaves £13.44. Note that cost of creation can be tricky: if you're bulk buying in sets of, say, 500, the 501st DVD can cost a lot more to create if you didn't order a whole second batch.

I've mentioned it before but this feels like a good place to bring it up again: remember to check if sales taxes apply to what you're doing. For example, if you're a UK company that turns over more than £85,000 a year you have to charge your customers VAT at 20%.

Figure 5.8 shows how this changes your calculations. You have to take off £5.80 VAT right away, which means you end up with only £9.44 in profit, less than half the actual reward level.

SHIPPING YOUR REWARDS

Research the shipping costs carefully. On most sites you can set the terms of where you're willing to ship to. Often you can also add a shipping surcharge that differs depending on where the backer lives.

On Kickstarter there are three options:

- **No Shipping.** Used for rewards like digital downloads or access to protected content. You'll need to provide a download link, password or code, so consider how you'll actually send these out. If you're aiming for thousands of backers, you can't physically do it yourself.

You could outsource this to your team or to a third party supplier like BackerKit, or set up an autoresponder on an email account.

- **Restricted.** Restrict shipping to only the countries you define. This can frustrate excluded backers, but it may not be physically possible for certain rewards to be shipped internationally (or may not be legal in some countries). Consider making tailored rewards for other countries so they don't feel left out and be sure to be very clear in the reward description. If you can, explain why a reward is restricted, especially if it is due to legal issues, as people will likely understand your choice.

- **Shipping Worldwide.** You set a global shipping rate and can pick different rates for certain countries (e.g. $20 to ship worldwide, but only $10 for countries in the EU). This extra amount is added to the backer's total at the checkout. It's important you do your research on costs before you set the shipping rates for each country. If you get this wrong it can start to add up quickly and cut your profit margin down.

IDEAS FOR REWARDS

Figure 5.9 has four groups for reward ideas. These are just rough groups based on what people want in return for their contributions. They are **community**, **shopping**, **the film** and **marketing**. Community rewards are for people who want to feel included. Shopping rewards are for those who want something more transactional. 'The film' is for rewards closely related to the actual film. And marketing rewards are those that will

	Community	Shopping	The Film	Marketing
	Thank you and shout-out	Digital products, like video files or soundtrack	Download of the script	You becomes a Lord in the world of the movie
	Access to the production diary videos	T-shirt, poster, badges	DVD of your previous films and early DVD	Psychic reading based on a picture of your elbow
	Dinner with the cast and crew	Merchandise package with mug, t-shirt & tote bag	Associate producer credit and early screening	Skype call with one of the animal stars
	Be in the film as an extra	One-off, unique items such as the clapperboard	Executive producer credit and festival screening	A character based on you is written into the movie

FIG 5.9 IDEAS FOR REWARDS

create a buzz about the film and give journalists something to write about. Of course, they need to be interesting rewards for the backers, too.

In each group we have four different levels of reward. Tier 1 might be around $1–10. Tier 2 could be up to around $100. Tier 3 could be from $100 to the low thousands. Finally, tier 4 could be thousands of dollars in value. Here are some examples of rewards in each category and for each tier.

COMMUNITY

- A thank you or shout-out
- Access to video production diaries
- Dinner with the cast and crew – if it's a particularly fun or large crew you could even have a big dinner party, but make sure it's clear who's picking up the cheque, and what travel arrangements need to be made
- Opportunity to be an extra in the film, or an executive producer credit

SHOPPING

- Digital products like video files, soundtrack (if you have the rights) or a copy of the script
- Physical products like T-shirts, posters or badges
- A merchandising package with lots of products bundled together, perhaps in a tote bag
- Unique, one-off items like the clapperboard from the shoot or something signed by the cast – whatever it is, it needs to be something special and different to the rest of your offers

THE FILM

- A download of the script
- DVDs of previous films or an early copy of the new one
- Associate producer credit or an invitation to the premier
- Executive producer credit or an invitation to film festival screenings

MARKETING (MY FAVOURITE)

- Be named a 'lord' in the world of the movie or something similar – useless but fun, like the way people sell plots of land on the moon

- Something wacky and strange, like a psychic reading based on a picture of your elbow

- Skype call with an animal star – a ten-minute call with a star hamster!

- A character based on you or a person you choose will be written into the film (being careful to avoid any lawsuits, of course)

TIPS FOR CREATING REWARDS

1. Crowdfunding is all about community, which is why popular rewards include:

   i. Access to project development
   ii. Opportunities for involvement
   iii. Limited edition products

2. Your core reward is access to your finished film. Be careful not to price this too low.

3. Consider early bird offers and limited numbers of rewards.

4. Create an additional reward for all backers when you hit a certain milestone. For example, once you reach your goal, perhaps everyone gets a free set of stickers. Remember to budget these out.

5. Immediate downloads increase trust as you will have already delivered on a promise.

6. Consider scalability. If you have 500 DVDs ready but sell 600, what will you do?

	KICKSTARTER	INDIEGOGO
Anything claiming to cure or treat illness	✗	✓
Drugs	✗	✗
Alcohol	✗	?
Energy food or drink	✗	✓
Financial incentive or profit sharing	✗	✗
Offensive material	✗	✗
Pornography	✗	✓
Air travel	✓	✗
Contests, lotteries or any kind of gambling	✗	✗
Resale	✗	✓
Weapons or ammunition	✗	✗
Political fundraising	✗	✓

FIG 5.10 PROHIBITED REWARDS

As a final note, you can refund individual pledges if you want. So, if you have a pledge from someone who is hassling you, or supports something you don't support, you can choose to decline their pledge.

PROHIBITED REWARDS

There are certain things you're not allowed to offer as rewards. Indiegogo is a little looser than Kickstarter but they could always change their rules in the future or on a case-by-case basis. If your whole campaign hinges on offering questionable or controversial rewards, I strongly suggest contacting them before you go full tilt into spending time and money.

Figure 5.10 shows some common restrictions for Kickstarter and Indiegogo. There are some things to be particularly careful of. You cannot buy products and then resell them as rewards (resale). Indiegogo does not allow rewards to be alcohol, although they can be tickets to an event that serves alcohol (which Kickstarter does not allow). Pornography is allowed on Indiegogo but not Kickstarter. Finally, if your film has a political bent, consider whether your campaign counts as political fundraising, which is not allowed on Kickstarter.

THE CAMPAIGN **VIDEO**

SHOULD YOU CREATE A VIDEO?

As a filmmaker trying to raise money for a film project, I'm sure you can imagine how critically important the main video you have at the top of your crowdfunding page is.

You can also embed other videos, further down the page, which you can use to explain the budget or introduce the team.

But that main video has to be the thing people are looking at and watching. It's your best chance to make your audience care about you and your project.

It also increases your chances of raising money. Indiegogo say campaigns with a pitch video raise 14% more than those without, and based on the research I did into Kickstarter film projects (shown in Figure 6.1), 91% of the successful ones had a video and 79% of the ones that failed didn't.

However, it is possible to launch a campaign without a video. If you're trying to raise a very

Projects with a video

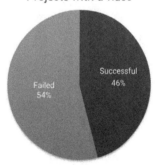

Projects without a video

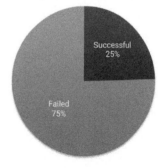

FIG 6.1 SUCCESS RATES BY WHETHER THERE IS A VIDEO

Pros of a video	Cons of a video
• It's the best way of proving you can make good films	• It could cost money
• You can entertain the audience, far better than text	• It could distract you from other opportunities
• You can better appeal to their emotions	• If you do it badly, you prove you can't make films
• It's the best platform to introduce yourself	• Campaigns do succeed without a videos
• Videos work	

FIG 6.2 PROS AND CONS OF A VIDEO

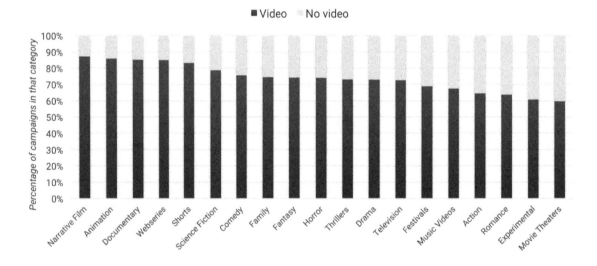

FIG 6.3 PERCENTAGE OF CAMPAIGNS WITH VIDEOS

small amount of money, or have another way of attracting and engaging your audience, you may want to skip over the time and money it will take to produce a video. Figure 6.2 summarises some pros and cons to using a video, and Figure 6.3 shows how the use of videos differs across project categories on Kickstarter.

CRAFTING A VIDEO MESSAGE WHICH WORKS

The starting point is to watch as many existing videos as you can. Every Kickstarter project is available for you to look at and, trust me, the more you watch, the more you'll get a real sense of what works and what doesn't.

The video has to look good. It is your strongest proof that you can and should make the final film.

The essence of a good video is to feature engaging people explaining their interesting journeys. Everything else is a bonus that makes it look better or be more entertaining. So don't be too ambitious and end up failing to meet the impossibly high standards you've set for yourself. It's much better to have a simple video made well than an audacious idea you don't quite pull off.

The campaign video has to be perfect for your crowdfunding pitch, which means it doesn't necessarily have to be in the same style as your final film. So even if you're making an animation, you may find a live-action video of you speaking to camera would be best.

You could use:

- **Live action reality**, which could be you or your team speaking to camera

- **Live action fiction**, which could be a trailer of your film or even a little short film in itself to explain why you need funding

- **Animation** or **graphics** with voiceover, which might be easier than actually shooting something

Start with your Post-it from earlier and focus on the key pieces of information you need to convey to tell your story and make people care about it.

Script and storyboard it to ensure it flows and is concise. You'll rework this a number of times. Whenever you have a draft, perform it to the mirror and then to friends to see how it sounds. It's very easy to think you can just do it off the cuff and improvise, but if you do that you might find it's not focused and ends up being longer than required. Trust me, I know from making these videos that the best thing I can

do is perform it a number of times, then write it down, script it, edit it, and finally perform it in a better form.

The most effective crowdfunding videos are those with people speaking honestly and openly to the camera. If you work as a team, you should pick the most likeable, charismatic person to present. Ultimately, the viewers need someone to be the main presenter, and that should be someone they will instantly warm to.

The aim is to make an emotional connection as soon as possible, so don't start with shots of trees and establishing shots. Go in there quickly and try to make people like you.

Eye contact with the camera will help a lot because it's eye contact with the viewers.

Use a conversational tone and not an infomercial business pitch. You're not talking to investors, or your boss; you're talking to your friends and people you hope will become your friends. When you're writing and performing it, picture yourself explaining the project to an old friend over a cup of coffee at the kitchen table.

Spend more time talking about why you're doing it rather than what you're doing. Don't spend time explaining the detail of the schedule, the cameras you're going to use or which video codec you'll be using for the YouTube upload. Focus on what it means to have this film funded. There's a great TED talk called 'Start with Why' which will help you really grasp this concept.

Sell the benefits to the backers. It's not all about why you need the money; it's about why they should support you. Go back to our reasons why people fund crowdfunding campaigns and see if you're addressing what your audience needs to know to get them onboard.

Remember at the end to have a clear and passionate call to action. It's so easy to make a film about your campaign, but then forget to actually ask for the money or support.

THE SOUND

Having watched quite a few Kickstarter videos, there's something I want to spend a little bit of time talking about: the sound. Most filmmakers already have an advanced knowledge of what makes a good image, and if you don't, there's no end of people who can help. However, sound is one area that's all too often overlooked, yet it's at least half the battle when it comes to making a video feel professional.

So here are some tips:

- Use a good directional microphone pointing at whoever's talking.

- Everyone who's speaking must have a microphone on them, or pointed at them

if it's directional. If you only have one microphone, do things in multiple takes. Do close-ups and wides or at the very least try ADR where you go into a quiet space and re-record the dialogue. It's never going to sound as good as location sound, but ultimately, if the location sound is bad or something is captured badly, you may not have a choice.

- Add music in the background, just subtly, as it adds to the professionalism. Make sure it's loud enough but that the music doesn't overpower the speech. Your video is fundamentally about one human being talking intimately to another, rather than trying to have a conversation in a loud nightclub.

- When using music, make sure you ask permission from the music owners. You'll need to get permission from all the rights holders, create it yourself or use a royalty-free

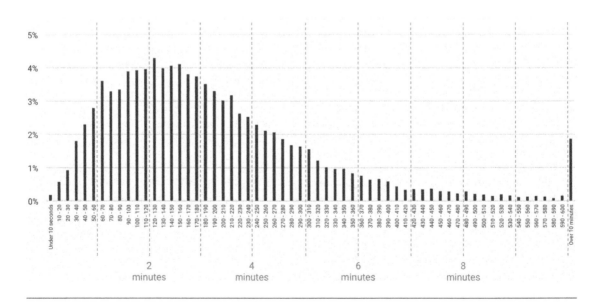

FIG 6.4 THE AVERAGE LENGTH OF CAMPAIGN VIDEOS ON KICKSTARTER

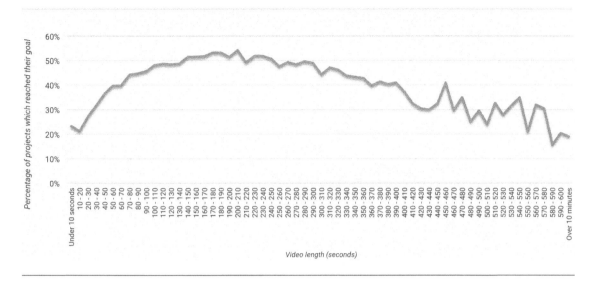

FIG 6.5 SUCCESS RATES OF CAMPAIGNS BY VIDEO LENGTH

music library where you pay one fixed fee and can then use it as you want.

HOW LONG SHOULD YOUR VIDEO BE?

There is no magic length that applies to everyone. It's very possible to make a minute-long video that overstays its welcome, and it's also possible to make a ten-minute video that needs more in it.

Looking at the statistics I've discovered on Kickstarter (see Figure 6.4), the majority of videos are around two minutes long, and the median length is 168 seconds, which is almost three minutes long. I'd say that's enough time to introduce yourself, make a case and then make a speedy exit before you overstay your welcome.

See also Figure 6.5 for data on how video length relates to success on Kickstarter.

TECHNICAL REQUIREMENTS

Some technical advice for your video:

- Don't leave it till the last minute.

- Run a test. It's very easy to run a dummy campaign that doesn't even get published, and as part of this you should upload a test video to see how it looks and how it compresses.

- With Indiegogo you can create a custom overlay, which is the image people see before they hit play. You don't have to make it look like some random clip from your film; you can actually upload something specific. The overlay you use for this is the same one used when you share the video on Facebook, so bear that in mind. You can update the image as the campaign grows, allowing you to add 'only a few days left' or tell the viewer the project is a staff pick.

K Kickstarter	GO Indiegogo
Hosted by Kickstarter.com	Hosted on YouTube or Vimeo
They create a 640 x 480 version (4:3 ratio)	MOV, MPEG4, MP4, AVI, WMV, FLV, 3GPP
MOV, MP4 or WMV	Overlay should be PNG or JPEG
5 gb limit	Overlay should be 640 x 427

FIG 6.6 TECHNICAL REQUIREMENTS FOR KICKSTARTER AND INDIEGOGO

The difference between Indiegogo and Kickstarter is that, with Kickstarter, the video is hosted on their site whereas Indiegogo ask for a YouTube or Vimeo link for them to embed. Figure 6.6 summarises some of the technical details.

THINGS TO BE MINDFUL OF

Here are a few last tips for when you're making your video.

Remember the first few shots are key. People judge based on first impressions so make sure you get quickly into the action, into the emotion and into the connection. Start with yourself.

If you can, avoid contentious topics such as politics or religion. Obviously, if they're part of your campaign, you're not going to have a choice. It might be one of the strengths of your campaign that you're making a bold statement. But if you're not, avoid that. It's not worth annoying people or turning them off.

Your sense of humour might not be to everyone's taste, so bear that in mind. Make sure you road-test the draft of the script and then the draft of the video.

A campaign with a small goal can get away with a lower-quality video. If you're trying to raise a few thousand dollars, you don't have to spend a further few thousand dollars making an incredibly high-quality video. You can do it with your phone or on a laptop, something basic like that.

However, if you're one of those campaigns trying to raise a lot of money – say, greater than $10,000 – you really do need a good video. There's no excuse. It doesn't have to be the most entertaining video of all time, but it must look great. If the sound is bad, no one is going to believe in your ability to make a good film.

Your campaign is most likely to succeed when you convince people who have no prior connection with you, so avoid in-jokes, local references or anything that needs explanation. You want to make everyone feel instantly included.

If you do have a strong accent don't be afraid to add subtitles. It's not an insult, simply about trying to reach more people, and Kickstarter actually allows you to upload your own subtitles – in fact, they say it's actually required if the main video is not English, French, German or Spanish.

MARKETING AND **PROMOTION**

MARKETING YOUR CROWDFUNDING CAMPAIGN

Marketing is key to the success of your crowdfunding campaign. You can't just rely on your friends or the filmmaking community. There are so many Kickstarter campaigns for films at the moment; the fact you're making a film isn't interesting in and of itself.

You need to use marketing to reach new people and communicate both who you are and why it matters that you make this film.

Kickstarter say only 5% of traffic to campaigns comes from people browsing the Kickstarter website. Indiegogo say 30% of money raised comes from the creator's own network. The rest will come from new people, and whether you attract them or not is all down to marketing.

Coordinate all the people working with you. Make sure they all know their roles, and how they fit into the marketing efforts.

SCHEDULING

It's important to build marketing into your schedule. Just as you schedule your whole campaign, do a smaller, more detailed version of that just for marketing.

You want new and interesting things to say throughout the campaign and that's hard to do off the cuff. There is only so long that your main message can be 'Gimme some money'!

Promote different aspects every week, or day even, to keep the messaging fresh. So, today you might be focusing on the science part, tomorrow it might be on the rocket, another day it might be on the characters. Obviously, this all comes from your overall pitch, which should relate to the Post-it note you have stuck on your monitor.

Note that journalists prefer to be involved with a campaign before it goes live as it gives them a better story and more privileged access, so make sure you schedule that in. If you've got really interesting story exclusives, consider carefully who the best person is to seed them with and at what point in the campaign it should be done.

SOCIAL MEDIA

You can use services like Hootsuite or Tweetdeck to queue up non-topical social messages. This means the main effort you really have to put in during the campaign, when it comes to social media, is saying hello and thank you to people and giving updates about things that have emerged during the process.

MARKETING OPPORTUNITIES

So, we need a plan for how we're going to get our awesome pitch in front of the right audience.

There are a number of marketing methods you can choose from. These include:

- **Email.** It may feel like it's an old method but top marketers continue to rely on it.

- **Social media.** This is split into two types:
  - Your network, i.e. the people you already know and who know you
  - Communities interested in your topic

  You need a different approach for each of these two audiences.

- **Outreach.** This is where you're working to get influential sites and people involved in the campaign.

- **Paid advertising.** This is paying for ads to appear to targeted communities around the web.

We'll be going through all of these methods over the course of this section.

EMAIL MARKETING

Email is the most personal way of marketing to people online. Way before the campaign launches you should be collecting email addresses from your address book, and from those of the people on your team.

Put them together into lists, carefully prioritising each person – how likely are they to give money and how likely are they to help promote the campaign? There are some people whose network and reputation are worth far more than their 20 bucks.

It sounds a bit mercenary but consider people's disposable income and what else they spend their money on. People with the highest income who spend money on hobbies or make purchases to improve their social status should be seen as high-value prospects.

This can take longer than you think because you forget just how many people you've met and have details for.

The most influential people in your community should get the most personal contact. Perhaps even a phone call. You can't do this with everyone, but this is all happening in the weeks leading up to your campaign launch, so you do have more time than during the actual campaign.

You can **mail merge** on Outlook/Excel or Gmail, meaning you can reach more people. Using mail merge also allows you to personalise your approaches – the opening salutation as well as the first few lines of the email can be tailored to that person.

Be careful of send limits. On Gmail it's about 2,000 emails a day and if you do more you can come across as spam.

You may wish to use a mail listing service such as MailChimp, AWeber or MailFlow. These can help you manage sending out large numbers of emails and also let you see who's opening them. However, make sure you have people's permission to add them to a list and make sure you account for the costs of these services in your overall budget.

Let's look at what you're writing in these emails.

The shorter the better.

Make sure they're open, personal and warm and avoid sounding like spam at all costs. We all know what spam sounds like: it's not personal, it sounds generic and we are turned off almost instantly. If you're not sure about the difference, read all the emails you had today; you can easily tell by the tone which are from friends and which are spam.

Make sure you mention how supporting your project helps them, not you. It's not really about you, it's about them.

Ask them specifically for what you want from them. If you just say 'We need support', it's a bit generic and they may not know what kind of support you need.

Hi Ed

I wanted to let you know about our new crowdfunding campaign. Please check it out and let me know what you think and/or support the film.

It's at www.example.com/projecttitle.

Thanks,
Stephen

Hi Ed

I was hoping you could help me with something. We've just launched our crowdfunding campaign and right now I need some feedback.

We're raising the budget to make our comedy feature film set in our town, so I want to make sure it appeals to people who know the area (i.e. people like you and I!).

Could you spare a couple of minutes to have a read and let me know what you think?

It's at www.example.com/projecttitle.

Thanks a million,
Stephen

FIG 7.1 EMAIL EXAMPLES

Hi. This is LOuie. It seriously is me. Im even going to leave the O stuipdly capatalized because who would pay an intern to do that?? Okay so you bought the thing with my fat face on it and you clicked the button that said i could email you. And i know that now you are thinking «aw shit. Why'd i let this guy into my life this way?». Well dont worry. Because i really swear it that i wont bug you. I will not abuse this privalage of having your email. You wont hear from me again... Probably, unless i have something new to offer you. The reason i'm writing now, in the back of a car taking me to the Tonight Show set, is to let you know that as of now there is some new and cool stuff on my site, related to Live at the Beacon Theater. Theres a thing where you can download and print a dvd box cover and label so you can burn and make your own dvd of the video. And theres a new option where you can gift the special to as many people as you want (for 5 bucks each) and they'll get a nice gifty email from you with a link to the video.

Also, some of you may know, i recently made a statement (that sounds so dumb. Like i'm the president or something) about how the video has been doing online. Im pasting it in here below in case you missed it.

Lastly I'm planning to put some more outtakes of the show on youtube and i think i will put one on the site that is only available for free to you folks on this list, who bought the thing and opted in. But dont hold me to that because really i just thought of it and typed it.

Okay well please have a happy rest of the year and more happy years after that. And please even have been happy in your past.

What?

Thanks again for giving me 5 dollars. I bought 3 cokes with it.

Regards. Sincerely, Actually,

Louis

FIG 7.2 OPENING TEXT OF A LOUIS CK EMAIL

Give them a single link in the email to channel them towards the campaign page. Don't give them a chance to get lost in a choice of what they click.

Try asking for advice. We talked about this earlier. Ask for money, get advice – ask for advice, get money.

See Figure 7.1 for a couple of examples.

The first example is very small and not very personal. It might be suitable for people with a short attention span, but you'll want something longer and more personal for other people.

You might also add an opening line, like 'Oh, I haven't seen you for weeks' or 'Go Mets'. Whatever the personal thing is, it's going to remind them you're a human being with whom they have a relationship.

If you want to have a look at an absolute genius, down-to-earth guy, take a look at the emails Louis CK writes.

Louis CK is a comedian who sold a video of one of his shows directly to the public. He doesn't send messages to his fans very often but when he does they always come across as human, personal and spoken from the heart.

Figure 7.2 is the opening text of an email he sent.

SOCIAL MEDIA MARKETING

Your social media outreach needs to be built over time. Get to know the communities and try to bring value to their worlds way before you start asking them for money.

Talk to people the way you do to friends. You wouldn't bombard a friend with generic marketing messages, I hope!

Be generous and try to pay into the communities with advice and promotion of other people's

work. Hopefully, if you're speaking with the right people, your audience will actually benefit from hearing about the other campaigns.

You could offer some of the best rewards as prizes to community members, although make sure you budget for this as you don't want it to get out of hand. Similarly, if there is a unique and large enough community, consider creating new rewards targeted at their members.

Share with people how it's going, especially your successes. Try not to let people know about your failures, although don't whitewash the complete journey as otherwise it'll sound both boring and a little like a North Korean government message!

Use a URL shortener so you can measure the impact.

Indiegogo have a nifty referral contest system that lets you give out different URLs to different people and then track how much money has been given via each one. That way you can track which of your champions has made the most impact in terms of helping you reach your overall goal.

INFLUENCERS AND MESSENGERS

One of the marketing methods open to you is outreach. This is a way of spending time and energy trying to connect with influential people who have an audience. You're not paying these people but it may cost you some money (and time) to reach them.

Finding the right gatekeepers will provide two things for your campaign:

- **A wider audience**, since you can reach the people they are communicating with

• **Credibility**, since when you have certain taste-makers promoting your campaign, or even just mentioning it, it seems more legitimate

Start by seeking out bloggers and journalists who've previously covered the subtopic featured in your campaign pitch. Pay special attention if you see they've promoted other crowdfunding campaigns – when you look at those campaigns, see how many were funded. You can't be certain it was all down to these people but it's a good sign that they're worth focusing on.

It might be worth contacting the filmmakers behind the previous campaigns to ask how they got in contact with particular bloggers. Did it go well? Was he/she useful?

When you talk to people, prove that you know their work or their topic; make sure it feels personal. You should contact these bloggers and journalists via private messages rather than leaving them public comments. Public comments can look a little desperate and may not work.

You should be doing this before you actually launch your campaign. Make them feel like they're in the loop. If you come to them in the middle of a campaign, and you've only raised a small amount of money, it's not going to look great and they won't have a reason to come onboard.

Be polite but persistent. There's no harm in writing a few emails to the same person. Not within the hour or on the same day, but perhaps every week or so if you need to, saying 'Oh, did you get a chance to see any of my messages?' Give them updates – this person's come onboard, the campaign's doing great, etc. Keep them onside.

If you don't ask you don't get, so even if you think there's no chance in the world they're going to read your email, still do it. What's the harm? We're talking about a little time and an email isn't the worst thing in the world.

USING BLOGS TO WIDEN YOUR AUDIENCE

When looking for the right news sites to contact, concentrate on the ones in your subtopic. Remember, you don't necessarily need a big audience but you do need a motivated one. Huge media publications probably won't cover you and even if they did it might not make much of an impact on pledges.

Remember to ask them to share on social media. Many forget this unless you specifically say 'Please can you share it?', especially on launch day. Let's say you got in contact with them a couple of weeks beforehand and they are keen to help you. The day before the launch you tell them 'Hey, Jeff, just remember tomorrow is the launch date', and on the launch day 'Hey, Jeff, it's today, so let's go'.

How do you get on the radar of these bigger news sites? Well, if you contact only big sites you're probably going to be lost in the crowd, whereas if you can find a very small niche blog they may be really interested in listening to you.

You need impassioned people, people who believe what you believe. Look for the smaller blogs that break big stories, and if you have the time, work backwards from news stories on the big news sites and look for who originally broke the news. There may be a link to the original piece or you may have to use Google. If you do this a number of times you might find the same small pool of bloggers coming up again and again.

You'll find that with film data. I do lots of early stage research into film data and statistics, and there are certain publications, including big ones like the *Guardian*, that may use my stories as the basis for big articles.

This is a technique that's very well explained in a book by Ryan Holiday called *Trust Me, I'm Lying*. I strongly recommend that you read this book as it's all about how to play the game of getting bloggers involved.

You can offer these sites exclusive information, and if you've got big stars coming onboard, allowing them to break the news might be worth a lot to them. Give them access to your teams, to do interviews or guest posts. Reciprocal promotion can benefit both of you, as can tailored rewards.

ONLINE LIVE EVENTS

Another form of outreach can be online events that create a buzz.

Reddit have 'ask me anything' threads which can give you a lot of attention if you have someone famous or a top expert in their field.

For example, if your campaign is about rocket ships and you have an ex-NASA engineer as an adviser, ask them if they're willing to answer questions for an hour or two. You can even offer to do the typing for them!

You can run chats offering advice on Twitter, Google Hangouts or a YouTube live stream.

Offer to take part in relevant podcasts that share the same audience you're trying to reach. Try contacting them and saying 'Hey, we have this campaign coming up in a few weeks. Can we meet with you?' or 'Would you like to interview us?' or 'Would you like to interview our star or expert?'.

OFFLINE LIVE EVENTS

Don't forget offline events as well, like a launch party to celebrate the start of the campaign.

These can be effective, although don't take your eye off the ball; perhaps the launch event should happen on the second or third day. That way, on the first day you can focus purely on online marketing. The better you start off on the first day, the more likely it is that you'll be ranking high on the Kickstarter algorithm and so be on their front page.

Alternatively, task a few people with completely running the live launch event so you only need to turn up, say a few words and then get back to your online marketing.

Fundraising parties and events can be powerful, especially if you feel your community isn't one you're going to reach online.

Try live streaming the best offline events via a service like Periscope so everyone feels included.

Offer to give talks to large communities like film clubs, conferences and meet-ups.

Old-school print marketing may also be useful. For example, you could try handing out flyers or getting local businesses to put up posters. The more local your campaign is, the more effective this will be.

Finally, consider telephoning key backers or gatekeepers. Now, you obviously have a limited amount of time unless you scale up. Think about how American election campaigns raise money. They have a whole bank of people on the phones, calling people up; you might want to do that. You don't want to spam anyone, but if you already have a reason to contact lots of people, maybe you could hire a couple of extra bodies to help. In my experience, actors and actresses tend to work really well because they're very good at playing a role and are able to constantly keep up their energy and excitement.

PAID MARKETING

As well as email, social media and outreach, you might want to consider paid marketing.

Online advertising is a huge business and it's not possible to cover it all in a short book like this. This overview is simply designed to be an introduction to the ideas.

If you're running a very small campaign, it's not likely to make financial sense to be doing this. But for larger projects, it might be a vital way of achieving three things:

- **Scale.** If you know you've got a great campaign which converts viewers into backers, but you're not getting enough people on the page in the first place, paid advertising can increase your traffic.

- **Reach.** You may be speaking to a fairly closed set of communities and so you want to branch out to people and places you have no prior connection with.

- **Targeting.** You can be highly specific about who sees your adverts, when and how. This means you can go after the very specific subgroups of people who are most likely to be excited about your campaign.

There are so many ways of spending money with advertising online so I've picked the five which are most likely to apply to you:

1. **Facebook** has one of the most targeted advertising platforms at the moment as they know so much about their users. You could run straight-up adverts or you could create content, such as articles and videos, and then promote that. In my experience, promoted content is much cheaper to run than a direct advert and has the advantage that some people will choose to share it for free. See if you can write something that will be of value to the audience for your subtopic.

2. **YouTube pre-roll advertising.** These are the video ads on YouTube which you can skip after five seconds. These can be quite cheap, at around $0.10 per play (i.e. the viewer watches beyond the skippable button), and they're also highly targeted. The more specific your target audience, the more you can expect to pay per view. They allow you to target very specific things, such as a zip code, so for a local campaign this could be a fun way to engage people who aren't used to seeing local ads on YouTube.

3. The ads you see on Google searches are organised through the same system as the YouTube pre-rolls, namely the **Google Adwords** platform. You can use this to target certain people, certain search terms or place ads on sites on a particular topic. The platform is free to use (you only pay when you actually run an advert) so I recommend you log on and see what it's like. It's helpful for your budget as you can use it to run one or two ads for a dollar or so, and use that to see how much it would cost you to scale up your marketing.

4. **You could advertise on Reddit.** You need to be a little careful as Reddit communities are really protective, so if you have a campaign that annoys them or they think you're taking advantage of them, it could backfire. But obviously, Reddit is one of the most trafficked

websites in the world and has quite a big, engaged, tech-savvy audience.

5. In recent years we've seen a boom in **paid crowdfunding PR consultants**. Regardless of whether you hire one, soon after you launch your campaign you're going to start getting private messages from consultants offering their services. My advice would be to research them way before you launch your campaign and to chat to some of their past clients. Don't hire someone at the last minute or purely because they spammed you on your Kickstarter page. A paid consultant can take 5–10% of your campaign funds, and maybe more. You should be careful what arrangement you make with them and how much work they can put into it.

Be selective about your audience; don't try promoting to everybody. Think what kind of audience is most likely to be excited by your campaign and who will turn into backers. This last bit is key – each new lead is costing you money so you need to be fairly certain they have the cash and ability to become a backer.

Narrow down your focus so you seem less generic to your audience. Rather than advertising on the word 'Shoes', run specific ads for each type of shoes.

Try a lot of different content and measure how it performs. Then double down on what works.

In the weeks leading up to your campaign you might want to write a few articles on your subtopic, promote them and see how they perform in small advertising tests to your audience. Look to see which create the highest engagement rates and try to figure out why. What is it in the successful articles that is inspiring the audience to take action? If you can figure this out, you may have learnt the secret to engaging your audience.

You must be sure to track the impact somehow. Look at conversion rates, how much you are spending, or how many people clicked on the article – whatever is the right metric for you. Otherwise you're just wasting your money as you'll never know how it helped you.

I recommend starting with small amounts of money to micro-test your adverts. It's very easy to spend a lot of money without even thinking.

RUNNING YOUR CAMPAIGN

JUST BEFORE YOU LAUNCH

You've planned your strategy, you've got all your elements together and are only days away from launching. Take a deep breath – your time is about to be taken away from you.

A few last-minute tips before you start:

- Make sure everyone in your team knows their role and knows the campaign inside-out. You can quiz them on it; make sure they can reel off all the advantages of being a backer and all the things that make your campaign cool, innovative, fresh and different.

- Run through who replies to which messages. So, who's going to thank the backers when they leave a message, who's going to thank the people who leave comments, etc.? You can't leave it up to chance and you don't want anyone to get ignored.

- Create a shared Dropbox with all the images, interviews and anything else you've created around the campaign. Make sure it's organised. Speaking as a filmmaker and someone who's done this before, a well-organised Dropbox shared among lots of people is very valuable. One big dump where everyone changes and renames files is not.

- Have all your assets prepared before the launch. This includes news and non-topical messages you'll be announcing later in the campaign.

- Prepare interviews that can be given to journalists as exclusives or put on to your campaign page. If you're giving them as an exclusive, make sure only one person can sign off on who gets them; otherwise two people in your team might sell the same exclusive to different publications.

- Generate ideas for interesting update videos which are surprising and interesting. That way, when you do updates during the campaign, you won't have to sit there thinking them up from scratch. You can't record them because you won't know in advance exactly what you're going to say in the update, but you can definitely prepare.

GETTING APPROVAL ON KICKSTARTER

The process of getting approval on Kickstarter is straightforward (see Figure 8.1). When you've finished creating your campaign you submit it. The Kickstarter algorithm checks it against their idea of a suitable project, looking at things like the product description, the rewards, the funding goal and whether the creator has launched a product in the past. If they're comfortable it matches their criteria, you'll see a 'Launch Now' button, which you can click when you want.

Otherwise they'll send you through to a manual review process. This takes around two working days.

Even if you're offered the 'Launch Now' button, you can choose to go to manual review to gain valuable staff feedback. I strongly recommend you take this as it's free feedback from people who really know what they're doing. Hopefully, you will have submitted your campaign well in advance of the planned launch date, so you'll have spare time anyway.

Kickstarter says about 80% of their projects which are manually reviewed are approved. The rest need changes or are refused for some reason.

FINAL CHECKS

Next come the very final, final checks.

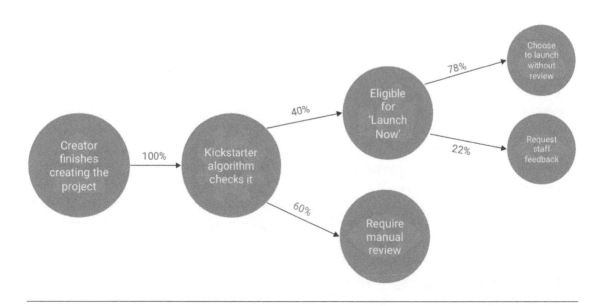

FIG 8.1 THE KICKSTARTER APPROVAL PROCESS

Have you completed your creator profile page? This is the bit where you explain who you are, and when people click on your name as a creator, that's where they'll be taken.

Test all the links on every piece of work you've put out there. You can't afford to be losing traffic.

Check you have permission for everything you're using: pictures, video clips, music. You don't want them taken down for any reason.

Have you updated your budget so you can afford any outcome? Think about it: if you're using a flexible-funding model to try and raise £10,000 and end up raising £5,000, can you afford to complete the project with that amount or not? You have to work out where you draw the line and say 'Below this amount we shouldn't take the money'.

Get two different people to proofread your work for typos and the way it feels.

Kickstarter lets you share the link before the official launch. That allows you to keep bloggers and journalists and all sorts of other people related to your subtopic in the loop. This will do two things: it will get them excited and make them feel special and it will also help you catch glaringly obvious things you've missed, because they will come back and say 'Well, that's incorrect'.

Hopefully, by this point, you will have had your project pre-approved by Kickstarter, checked the details and know when you will start.

Breathe deep and get ready to launch.

WHEN THE CAMPAIGN IS LIVE

So now your campaign is live.

The first few days are going to be critical. Hopefully you've queued up a number of people to talk about the campaign and become backers. You're aiming to build a sense of momentum and an air of confidence.

If you're on Kickstarter, the algorithm picking which projects they feature on the front page favours those with momentum in the first few days. Plus, all of your audience will be encouraged when they see you're doing well. Not many people are willing to publicly support something they think is failing.

The first thing you need to do is send out the emails you've been preparing to your contact list. The first and second days may provide the highest per-day average for donations. Some people even put in their own money to get the ball rolling. Kickstarter doesn't allow this but Indiegogo does, as long as you don't use the same PayPal account. It's up to you if you want to do that or not. Indiegogo also allows you to add offline contributions to your campaign so you might be able to use that to kick-start it.

During the actual campaign, be prepared for the fact that money won't come in evenly. There will be low points where you think 'Oh my God, there's no way I'm going to make this goal', but stick with it. Keep grinding away. There are many people who'll hear about it and are thinking about donating but haven't actually done it yet. Keep promoting the campaign, even if you don't feel like it.

A slow start can still lead to success, especially if you keep on pushing. But if you give up it's definitely over.

Keep up with everyone who's helping you in any way so you can thank them later on, and keep pushing updates, keep answering questions.

Video updates are a really powerful tool in engaging your audience. You don't need to make them as slick and professional as the main campaign video, although you should obviously avoid things like bad sound and bad lighting. The most important thing is that they feel personal and capture the excitement and passion of the campaign.

Backers want to know what's going on. If you just take their money and ignore them, they're going to feel very left out. They might even demand the money they've pledged back.

Keep them onside with thanks and communication. These are the people keeping your campaign alive and making the project happen. So talk to them. There's also a chance you can turn them into ambassadors. They've already given you money but now they can help further by really pushing the campaign to their networks.

They might also extend their pledge. If you're close to your goal, contact your backers and say 'Hey, I know you've given me $20, but could you give me $30?'. On Kickstarter you're able to adjust your pledge up or down at any point during the campaign.

DEALING WITH SUCCESS

So, what if all goes well? What if you have a huge success? Brilliant! Your project goes viral and you're collecting money, contacts, updates and comments. You'll be a little overwhelmed, so prepare yourself for that. This is where your team comes in and can help you.

On the other hand, there will certainly be times in the campaign when you're bored, tired and frustrated. Remember to sleep, eat, go outside and talk to people. You need moments where you just clear your head and do whatever you want to do to recharge. Go for a run or a swim or whatever.

If you're struggling to keep up with the demands of the campaign, reach out to people to join your team, and in an emergency use services like People Per Hour (see below) to find a virtual assistant. They can reply to emails, social messages and log progress for a relatively low cost.

You can also pay for special help. You might need technical assistance if, for instance, your personal site is down and you don't know why.

TRACKING HOW YOU'RE DOING

Kicktraq has a great service to track your success and see how it's going. If you install a browser add-on you can see the funding progress for any other campaign out there. This will help you see how close you are to your goal and how this compares to similar campaigns. They also have good statistics for when you'll reach a certain point and when you're most likely to reach your target goal.

You can track the success you're having on social media with services like Buzzsumo, which can tell you the number of shares on Facebook, LinkedIn, Pinterest, Twitter, etc.

You can use Google searches to find out how many people are linking specifically to your URL.

You can set up Google Alerts so you get an email every time someone mentions a certain phrase specific to your campaign. Make sure to use the subtopics you're targeting. This allows you to jump on opportunities to promote your campaign through people writing new blog posts or commenting on relevant news stories around your topic.

STRETCH GOALS

Stretch goals are when you say what you'll do with money you raise over and above your original goal.

If you're trying to raise $10,000 in 30 days and you've achieved that, you can now say 'If we raise $12,000 we can shoot it in 3D'. Explain how this new money will be spent and make it clear this will be in addition to the original plan, not instead of it.

Stretch goals and new rewards based on success can be a powerful marketing tool, as they give people something new to talk about and it's exciting when you say 'Oh my God, I'm overwhelmed, thank you all so much'.

It's also a great media story because it's about success and the surprise of doing better than you thought you would. Remember earlier in the book, when we were talking about the challenge plot and how it inspires action? The guy who had a $10,000 Kickstarter campaign and has now raised $100,000 is an inspiring story; you'll find plenty of people who will want to cover it.

IN THE LAST FEW DAYS

As you get closer to the end, you need to be going on overdrive. The last four or five days are critical – make or break.

If people are interested but haven't given money yet, now's the only chance they will have. Let everyone know it's now or never. Add new rewards, ideally based on the feedback from your audience. For example, people might have said to you, 'I would have given you more if you'd had this.' Perhaps even ask your backers in one of your updates: 'What else would you like to see?'

Remember to budget and plan for any new rewards you announce. If you suddenly say 'Oh wow, we're making so much money I'm going to send everyone a new DVD', make sure you've budgeted for that.

You can change your title and thumbnail during the campaign so you might want to add time pressure to those.

If you're close, but worried about missing the goal, you can donate to your own campaign (Kickstarter doesn't allow it, Indiegogo does).

USEFUL SERVICES AND SITES

Most people assume when they start the crowdfunding process that it will be just themselves and maybe a couple of close collaborators. But if you want to raise a lot of money, you're going to need to use some third-party services.

All of these services charge money so why would you enlist outside support?

- You may be missing key personnel and there's no one in your location or network who can help.

- It might help plug a skills gap. The chances that you have all of the things you need in-house are pretty small, so rather than your project suffering for lack of one skill, you can go out there and find it in the commercial marketplace.

- It might allow you to scale up. Even if you can do every task yourselves, the limited time period might mean you need to use outside resources to get it all done in time.

- You can build upon other people's existing knowledge. If you hire an expert in Photoshop to create a couple of images, you don't need to waste time learning Photoshop – you can get the benefit of their years of experience.

- Finally, it can allow you to focus on what you do best, or what you enjoy. So, you might hate the process of organising Facebook adverts, for example, but there are people out there who are happy to do that for a living, or enjoy doing it. You can outsource it to them.

It's important you investigate your options way before launch. Even if you're not sure you're going to need an outside service, it really is worth checking out the sites I'm about to go through. Look at the options open to you, note down the interesting ones and have them as a 'break glass in emergency' option to whip out during the campaign if needed.

These are the services I think it's most useful for you to know about:

FIVERR

The first is Fiverr. It really is a simple site: everything costs $5. Well, actually, it doesn't. These days, there are many things costing more than $5, but that's where the name came from originally.

People offer services mostly, at extremely cheap rates.

- You might use them for help writing your campaign pitch.

- You might be able to get feedback. You say to someone 'Please watch my video, look at my campaign and give me some feedback'. For $5 that's definitely worth it if you find the right person.

- There are also promotional offers on Fiverr where people offer to promote your campaign.

Obviously, bear in mind that these aren't going to be high quality, but it could fit into a bigger plan to generate more awareness.

- There will be people on the site with graphic design skills that might help you.

- They can also create video elements. You don't really want someone to produce an entire video, but they might be very good at creating an animated logo, for example, or doing a professional voiceover.

- There is even one service where, if you give them $5, they'll donate $2 to your campaign and leave a comment. I can't imagine this is worthwhile in the long term because obviously you're losing $3 every single time, plus the Kickstarter fees/processing fees. However, if you feel you've got a small campaign and one thing holding you back is the number of backers, maybe you'd consider it.

PEOPLE PER HOUR

People Per Hour is a service I use a lot, and it's fantastic. It connects you with people who've got skills in all sorts of different areas.

There are two ways you can work with them – either you can browse specific services people are offering (called 'Hourlies') or post your own job and ask people to bid for it. Then you'll get a load of proposals from people, each explaining how they'd do it, how much they charge and why you should hire them.

You'll pay more than the people on Fiverr but the quality will be a lot higher. You might use it to:

- Outsource the writing of your campaign pitch to a copywriting expert.

- Get expert feedback, because there are some real experts on there.

- Have your subtitles translated into another language, or even get the whole campaign translated.

- Create very professional images and videos.

- Find someone to build your project website, instead of using a WordPress theme and the plug-ins I mentioned earlier in the book.

BACKERKIT

BackerKit was set up specifically to support crowdfunding creators. The founders had their own Kickstarter campaign and discovered it was actually very hard to send out all their rewards and manage the backers, so they created BackerKit.

When you've completed your campaign you export all of your backers' details from your crowdfunding platform and then upload them to BackerKit:

- You can use it to send backer surveys to all the people who have given you money. You just need to know their addresses and if they want the red or the blue T-shirt.

- They offer digital downloads. You can upload a single version of the film to BackerKit, and they will then manage the control, only giving it to your backers.

- You can opt to auto deliver rewards the instant someone makes a pledge, rather than waiting until the target has been reached. So, when somebody pledges money, they instantly get some kind of communication from you.

- They allow you to group backers and offer them different rewards or surveys.

- They allow you to automatically distribute codes, such as sending out a password, or unique game codes.

- One of their best features is that they also offer the backer a chance to add on an item when they've completed the survey. It's an extra sales opportunity where backers can buy more stuff from you after the campaign is over.

I strongly suggest that you check out BackerKit. It may or may not be right for you but it's definitely worth considering if you're going to have a large base of backers and need a way of managing them.

They currently charge a few hundred dollars to get set up, 1% of the amount you raised on Kickstarter and a further 5% of the funds you raise directly through them, via add-ons.

AMPLIFIER

Amplifier is a separate company from Indiegogo but they do have a strategic partnership.

You upload your designs to them and then they will print, pack and ship your rewards for you – meaning you don't ever have to physically touch them (the rewards that is, not the backers – although you don't have to touch them either!).

It's at its best when you have a medium-to-large number of rewards to send out as they have a minimum of about 100 shipments per campaign.

They offer T-shirts, mugs, mousepads, prints – all sorts of things.

Let me give you an example of the costs. For a one-colour T-shirt, they'll ship it within the US for just under $10. The order fee is $2.70 and then the postage and packing is just under $4. Which means that if your reward is $30, you know you're going to get $20 after all the fees are deducted.

This is for a one-item order and the cost would obviously be a lot less if someone ordered five T-shirts, or a T-shirt and mug, for example, because you're not paying repeat order fees. There are other minor costs like set-up fees but they're not huge.

GREEN INBOX

Green Inbox is a service that will generate messages for you on Facebook, LinkedIn, Twitter and via email. When you sign up for the service, you write what you want the message to say to people and then they will individually send each one, making sure they don't break the terms and conditions of each of those sites.

They charge you about $0.60 per Facebook message, but they have a money back guarantee as they can track how successful the campaign has been. They say 90% of their clients have reached their funding goal.

CROWDFUND BUZZ

CrowdFund Buzz is a good way to distribute press releases. They're not that cheap, charging from $250 up to about $650, but you'll get your own dedicated publicist and they know crowdfunding quite well.

AFTER THE CAMPAIGN IS OVER

So... your campaign has finished. Hopefully you've reached your goal but either way the

madness is over; the begging from all your friends, family and strangers over the last few months can finally stop.

The first thing to do is thank everyone, as personally as you possibly can. If there are 10,000 backers, of course you can't be personal, but there are ways you can pick the people who had the biggest influence and thank them personally.

If you only have a hundred backers, sit there and send each of them an email that uses their first name. That's a nice thing to do and if your whole team helps out, it's probably only an hour's work.

Make delivering your rewards a priority. People are quite impatient and they'll expect their rewards ASAP. They are focusing on themselves and not on the fact that you've got a thousand other rewards to send out. Be aware of that when they angrily email you asking how much longer it's going to take.

Kickstarter will send your backers a survey if needed, which can ask for additional information like their addresses, but you could also use an external company like BackerKit. BackerKit lets you have 'add-ons', which are items the backers can add at the checkout when they complete the survey.

Move updates from the crowdfunding page to your own site. The crowdfunding campaign page will be there for ever but it's not the best way to engage with your backers and fans in the future. So start shepherding them towards your project URL.

That said, don't forget to put some updates on the crowdfunding page even if these are mostly just links to your main blog. There are some people who will forget that link and go back to the crowdfunding page and see you haven't updated it for a while.

Pay any taxes due: sales tax, income tax, tax on profits, etc. After finishing the project, and spending all that money, you really don't want to fall foul of the taxman.

COPING WITH FAILURE

If you fail to reach your goal and are on a platform that allows flexible funding, you will still be able to receive the money that's been pledged. But you may or may not want it. If you've tried to raise $10,000, but only managed $500, you don't really want to take it as you have to deliver the rewards to those backers.

Even if your project fails, thank everyone who helped and donated. You may wish to run another campaign in the future for which these people could be key. Many people didn't support you but these people did.

Don't just abandon the campaign if you're in the middle and it's not working. It's horrible when you see a campaign that's just a wasteland; where the people behind it have said 'Oh, we're going to send you another update tomorrow', and that's where it ended two years ago. Be gracious, be polite, thank everyone.

LEVERAGING SUCCESS INTO A LONG-TERM COMMUNITY

Now the challenge is to build long-term relationships with your backers.

Keep in touch with them. Give them bonus rewards when possible. There may be many things you can do that are quite generous but weren't promised when your backers gave you money. Now you can add them in just because it's a nice thing to do.

Keeping their goodwill means everything.

If there's a problem, own up. Let people know what happened and, even if you haven't got a solution, talk to people, send updates and apologise.

If the worst happens and your project falls apart (which occasionally happens), be open about it. You might say: 'Look, guys, we raised $10,000, we thought that would be okay, but it turns out it's not nearly enough. We've only shot a third of the film and we can't shoot the rest of it. This is what we shot, we're very sorry, we hope you guys will forgive us.'

If you impress them by doing this, those people might be willing to become funders of your next project or give more money to finish this one. Honesty goes a long way, as does vulnerability.

Your backers could also be very useful for future negotiations when it comes to getting your film out there. Say you've had 1,000 people back your campaign. In a year's time, when the film is finished and you're trying to get a distributor onboard, you might be able to get those 1,000 backers to email people or tweet to show the film's appeal.

Promote your crowdfunding story to bloggers and journalists to keep up your profile. You may want to be running future campaigns and, if you're a filmmaker, you will almost certainly have a new film to promote at some point.

INTERVIEWS

ELLIOT CHAPPLE
MARKETING & DATA WIZARD
AT POZIBLE

STEPHEN: *How many films have been successfully funded on Pozible?*

ELLIOT: Looking at the information in the database it looks like we've funded 1,900 over the past five years, in the film or video categories.

STEPHEN: *And what kind of success rate does that amount to?*

ELLIOT: The film category success rate is 63%. We believe our success rate is much higher than other major platforms because we do a lot more hands-on work with the creators. We give every single campaign positive feedback on approval.

There's someone looking through the campaign and giving them good advice. And this information is based on all the campaigns we've ever seen. In conjunction with that we try to send out well-timed messages with the information campaigners need, depending on what stage they're at.

And also we offer services like a professional campaign adviser – you can talk to them about your campaign and ask questions along the way. So these are the main reasons why our success rate is much higher.

We really put our energy into educating people who want to run crowdfunding campaigns so that they know what they're getting into before they start.

STEPHEN: *Are there any common traits that we see in crowdfunding?*

ELLIOT: I guess, throughout the life of a campaign, there's always a lot of activity early and there's always a lot late.

So, early activity is when all the core supporters of the project are going in and pledging. The late activity is generally because it's people's last chance to get involved, so they're all jumping in and helping it hopefully get over the line with its target.

During the middle it can be quite quiet. So we don't generally see a trend there.

STEPHEN: So, what are some traits of the best crowdfunding projects? Do you have any tips based on what you've seen?

ELLIOT: I'd say a lot of the projects we approve, we see they have really in-depth information on their budget. This is really important because you want to instil confidence in your supporters, that the project is going to go ahead and you've thought of everything possible in terms of finance. A lot of projects forget to include really strong evidence of this, and also things like graphs and charts, they always work really well.

A lot of people also forget to include a nice visual element to their campaigns. You really want to keep people engaged. People don't really spend long on campaign pages on average so you really want to express the project as efficiently as possible. Using nice images and graphs and charts are all good ways of doing this.

The last thing is that it's really important you have rewards tiered in a few different amounts. We see $25, $50, $100 rewards as being the most popular and then going up into the hundreds or even thousands. So you really want to give people a good variety of choice as to what level they enter at to support the project, and well-balanced rewards.

CHRIS JONES
WRITER & DIRECTOR OF *GONE FISHING*

www.chrisjonesblog.com

STEPHEN: *Okay, Chris, so tell us a little bit about* Gone Fishing *and the origins of why you decided to make it?*

CHRIS: So, back in 2006, I think it was, I'd sent out a script to a major British producer who said, 'We love it, we want to make it, but we can only make it for $15 million, which means you can't direct.' Even though I'd previously made a bunch of feature films, they were all low-budget, very inspirational but certainly under a million dollars, way, way under a million dollars. And that meant I was unbondable.

And so I said in the meeting, listen, I know I'm the right person to direct this movie so I will prove to you by making a short film. I will make an Oscar-winning short film, I'll win the Oscar next year. Which, as soon as I said it out loud, I thought, oh my God, that's just insane, how am I going to do that?

Because winning the Oscar is not like winning the Olympics. I can't train and just be the fastest; it's ultimately other people who decide. You can't focus on an end point and say, 'If I do all of these things and I train and I train and I train, I can win. It's just very ephemeral, it's a competition, it's art, it's craft and it's down to other people's opinion and how that art and craft lands in their minds, in their subconscious, in their soul, however they define quality.

And at that time I didn't have the money to make it. But it had to be shot on 35, it had to look like 12 minutes of Harry Potter, that kind of scale. It had to be very, very impressive. And so I thought, I'm just going to ask everyone I know for £50. I started a blog (I didn't really have a blog at that point). I just put up a PayPal button and put it out there, and because I had the Guerilla Filmmaker's Handbook people I thought maybe I'd raise £5,000.

We kind of figured out we needed somewhere in the region of £12,000 to £15,000 and I was prepared to put a bunch of stuff on credit cards and do the usual anything. And very rapidly it kind of got traction and what people seemed to really enjoy was the journey. Because I was blogging every day about what was happening and I really committed to that and it wasn't just a 'this kind of happened today' blog. It was detailed analysis and really well thought through. People were able to emotionally go on the journey with me.

And then, when people started donating, it wasn't like a 'give me £50' button, it was like a 'give me anything you want'. So I was getting £1 and £5 and £50, most of them were £50 or £100, and then I started getting some big ones like £500 and £1,000. And then somebody gave me, completely out of the blue, £5,000, which was really surprising.

And the perks were, you know, everybody talks about the perks now, but there was the obvious stuff like get yourself a copy of the movie and all of that stuff. But I think the one that really excited people was, you can come to the after-party after the Oscars with me if we get to win. Anyone who knew me knew I'd give it my all, and I think most people who contributed believed there was a chance of this. It might have been a slim chance, but there was a real chance.

And actually, as a good friend of mine said, 'Are you kidding? £100? I get to go to a premier at BAFTA, I get to have a DVD with my name on it, and I get the possibility of going to an Oscars after-party in Los Angeles? That's insane value for somebody who doesn't have any connection with the film world.'

STEPHEN: So it was kind of a lottery ticket as well as real rewards. You said there was the film, signed posters, and a premier which were guaranteed, and then there was this lottery ticket.

CHRIS: Yeah, and that lottery ticket then started to act as an accelerant; it made me start to raise my game because now I just had to win the Oscar, I just had to because I'd committed to this. And then they could see I was taking huge amounts of action and throwing all my passion into it. So they'd come back and give me more money because they wanted me to win the Oscar.

And there were a couple of naysayers who would publicly say, 'You're an idiot, of course you can't win an Oscar, it will never happen.' Of course, all those people also said 'I knew it all along' when I got the email from the Academy saying, 'You're in the top ten, don't cancel February because you might be coming to the Oscars, and by the way you can't tell anybody. So yeah, we got Oscar-shortlisted, which meant we were the only British film in the top ten in the 2009 Academy Awards. It was unbearably exciting.

STEPHEN: I seem to remember you put it up on your blog and then they got back to you telling you to take it down? So there must have been a moment there, but from then onwards you had to keep tight-lipped, which isn't your style.

CHRIS: Yeah, because, effectively, I'd promised to blog the whole experience. And it all happened at the Bahamas International Film Festival where I'd just won best film and I was kind of floating around thinking, this is really awesome. I went upstairs, hit refresh on my email and then suddenly there's the email from the Academy going, 'Dear Mr Jones, good news, you're in the shortlist for the Academy Awards this year.'

I immediately got on the phone and rang everybody and I put it on the blog, and then I got an email saying take it down, take it down, take it down. So we quickly retracted it. I then put it back on the blog six months later after it wasn't news, with all the verification that I had that it was actually true. Because even then people were emailing me saying they didn't believe me, it wasn't true.

STEPHEN: It must have been quite a rollercoaster then, that you had to take it down and there was a chance you'd scuppered your chances. Paranoia always kicks in, you know. But let's get back to the beginning. I'm interested in your audience. So when you decided to do this and you put up your first blog saying, 'Hey, if you want to give me some money, this is how you do it,' what kind of audience did you have in scale and fervour? Because obviously it grew later on, but where did you start from?

CHRIS: Well, not social media. Twitter probably existed but I certainly wasn't on it. I might have got on it and had 11 followers, it was insignificant, and even Facebook, I'm not sure I even Facebooked a single thing, ever. It was literally from word of mouth, from people saying, there's this really cool thing, you should get onboard, and me emailing out to my email list, which was not big, it was 1,500 people, people that had come on a course or bought my books or had some kind of relationship with me. It wasn't very large at all.

But the word just spread and, again, it was quite an unusual thing. And a lot of smart filmmakers knew me, knew the opportunity and said, 'Oh, I get an associate producer for £50 on a potentially Oscar-winning film, that's an actually really cool IMDb credit.' Plus, I'd committed to run this two-day course about how we'd made the film. So, for the filmmakers, it's a pre-buy, how-to-win-an-Oscar course, for £50.

And I think that was the majority of our sales at the time. I don't think it would work today because most of that information is out there. I think it would work if a proper thought-leader, somebody who has already got a large audience and is already doing great stuff, announced they were going to do this incredible thing, whatever that thing was. They may be able to, but it definitely has shifted.

But interestingly, most of the people who contributed, outside of the emerging filmmaker sector, were older people. Older people who had families and saw us as an inspirational journey and wanted to go on that journey with us. People with disposable income, not necessarily rich, but who could afford takeout and would sacrifice this week's takeout for the potential of going to an Oscars after-party.

STEPHEN: So, would you say you had two audiences: a transactional audience who are looking at the rewards and financially calculating them, of course, and then an aspirational audience where it wasn't really about returns, it was about living vicariously through you?

CHRIS: Yes, definitely, and again they kept coming back because I shared all the data on the blog. The first festival we got into was Rhode Island. It was an Oscar qualifier, which meant if we won best picture there, we were Oscar-longlisted. So it was really important out of the gate, that we win. And so I thought, right, I've done everything up on steroids, I'm going to do this up on steroids, and we ended up with posters in the window at Starbucks. We did this really big campaign.

And the festival itself, run by George Marshall, recognised that it was Oscar-contender material and their audience is typically over 40 and they would probably warm to it. So we did a video blog. I went down to the local tech shop and bought a cheap video camera and said, right, we're going to video everything. I turned the camera on myself and said, right, we're at Heathrow Airport and we're going off here.

We made these videos and edited them every night. We'd go sit down at the computer and knock it all together, make this 15-minute, 20-minute thing, and we'd put it up on the blog every day. And that was when my blog went suddenly from 50 reads a day to around 1,000 a day, because suddenly it was like live television, people were coming back to watch the next episode of what was going to happen at the festival.

And we had two screenings. The first wasn't great due to a bunch of technical reasons, but then they gave us a second screening at the closing of the festival and there were 2,000 people present. And one of the traditions that's come out of *Gone Fishing* that I do at every screening now, is we thank the associate producers who are the contributors by giving them a big cheer and a round of applause when their name comes up. And it creates a magic moment, it's fun and everybody smiles and we all love it.

But that happened kind of spontaneously at the Rhode Island International Film Festival and the film is so feelgood and it so kind of resonated with the audience and them being American as well, it was a proper David and Goliath story for me. Also, the film is kind of that as well. Literally, there's a giant fish called Goliath, and they were all so rooting for me and the film made them feel so good, when the associate producer credits came up, it was suddenly like a Guns and Roses concert and everybody went mad. And it created this completely unforgettable moment that we captured on film.

And then, of course, all the people who'd contributed got to share in that moment on the other side of the world and it made them feel awesome and they continued on the journey with me for years and years. People who put in £50 were starting to buy 25 DVDs off me for Christmas presents. And that was how I was able to start funding the festival strategy. And even that, it cost me, I'm going to pull it out of my ass, but let's say £5,000 to do the festivals.

STEPHEN: And that wasn't in your original budget that you raised?

CHRIS: No, so I had to fund that somehow and I ended up funding it by selling the DVDs. I sold them at festivals but also to anybody in the UK, and I think we sold 1,000 DVDs in the first two weeks, just because people wanted a copy and wanted to share it, that was the key. They wanted to share it because it's not like... God bless independent film, but most independent film is a challenge. You don't give it to somebody going, here, watch this, and they go, thank you so much. It's like giving them a chore, a painful experience.

STEPHEN: Well, no one says, 'Let's grab some beers and some indie films.' It's not something anyone's ever said.

CHRIS: Exactly. Whereas *Gone Fishing* is very much a happy film and it's only 11 minutes long, 13 with credits. So it's not a big commitment for anyone and it felt like a Christmas present. And it just happened to land that I put the DVDs up sometime in October or November, so people were buying them for Christmas presents.

STEPHEN: Do you think your tone, when you teach and when people talk to you, but which also comes through in emails, is very conversational, very 'no nonsense' but also inspiring? Do you think that was a part of communicating your journey? That it's something other filmmakers should, not emulate, but find their own version of, this aspirational kind of honesty rather than some sort of slick advertising, with a slogan-heavy, corporate feel?

CHRIS: I always say, when people say, 'How do I get a job?' I'm always very clear: talent is great but relationships get you hired. And it's the same with crowdfunding.

People want a relationship with a person, they don't want a relationship with a film, a product or an organisation. They want a human relationship.

And for me, whatever happens on your journey is completely fine, whether the whole thing tanks and bombs in flames, it doesn't matter so long as you have the integrity and passion to communicate and say, we've just hit this extraordinary block and it's going to be very painful for a while. People then go, I'm behind you, I'm with you.

It's about having the integrity to share authentically and, whatever you commit to, to deliver what you commit to. I cannot tell you, 'I've stopped contributing to crowdfunding campaigns now because I'm disillusioned with the engagement after they've had my money.' It's like, guys, you took whatever it was, for me the cost of a Starbucks, or I believe in you a bit more and I gave you £50, whatever it was. I don't feel you're communicating the same level of passion.

And I have a suspicion that part of this is down to Indiegogo and Kickstarter because I get those branded emails, this is a project update from Kickstarter. I would rather have Jim from blah da blah saying, 'Guys, awesome news from my film.' Kickstarter just feels so impersonal and the system lends itself to that because it's so easy for the filmmakers to use. They don't have to manage their own email list and find a way of communicating more authentically.

STEPHEN: I suppose they can hide behind it a little bit because it's the system, it's the way you're supposed to do it, they're thinking about the journeys they're used to going on. I mean, I had a similar thing to you. I gave £30 to a theatre project a couple of years ago, a tiny amount of money, and I just thought it was interesting and I didn't know the people.

And the first email I got, beyond the automated 'here is a receipt for your thing', was about six months later, and I saw it was from the theatre company and I thought, oh, cool, they're belatedly thanking people or maybe there's another run or something like that. And it was another campaign they were running and they wanted more money from me.

And I was like, well, no, because you only got back in contact when you wanted more money from me and I thought about it afterwards, and actually I didn't need much from them. If they'd only sent me one or two emails saying thank you, giving a little update, I would have given them more money.

CHRIS: That's why I started a blog back in 2007. I said, 'I'm not going to clog your inbox but I want you to have a personal relationship with me. So go to my blog, once a week, once a day, whatever suits you, whatever level of communication you want, go to my blog, it's all there. What's happened in the last twenty-four hours, week, month, whatever you want, you can scroll down it, you can read stuff, you can watch videos,' and that really, really worked.

And people would email me and leave comments on the blog and I'd get back to them and comment back on the blog; that was very important as well. Human beings, we all communicate differently. Some people are obsessively tweeting me, and I'm like, the problem with a tweet for me is it's come and it's gone. And if I'm in the middle of a meeting and a tweet comes and it's gone in my feed, I'm not going to scroll back days and days to find that tweet.

The same with Facebook Messenger. The benefits are: it's immediate and it pops up. The downside of it is 24 hours later I've forgotten about it and it isn't in my inbox. So I think email is very important because you have to hit delete to get rid of one. Whereas many of the other social media things, they just disappear into the feed.

So I would say focus on email and give people the choice as to where they would like to connect, like here's my Facebook page, follow my fan page or group or however you want to do it, or even my own personal page; if that's the way they want to do it, fine. If they want to go to your blog, fine. Just make sure all the information is disseminated across all the platforms so that whatever their preference is, you're feeding that.

But ultimately I would funnel everyone back to a permanent blog. That also has the benefit that, a year later, people can Google you and they don't get taken to a Kickstarter page. And who knows what's going to happen to Kickstarter in five years or ten years. Your content is your content; you should own it.

STEPHEN: The last thing I want to talk to you about is storytelling. Obviously you're a filmmaker and a storyteller. One of the things that I remember, because we knew each other back then, is I would be reading your blog and I started to be pulled in as a fan because you would blog when you couldn't say something, when you couldn't announce something but you were excited. You would put up something saying, 'There's something happened that I can't tell you about for a while, a week, a day, or it hasn't happened yet and I don't want to jinx it, but I'm really excited.'

Basically there was this storytelling technique. And I remember calling you at least two or three times going, 'Look, I don't care what it is but I need to know what it is.' I couldn't deal with not knowing and I remember thinking, that's not something that I read a lot on blogs; there was too much of we did this or I think that. There was very little of 'There will be this', so it's that storytelling thing.

CHRIS: So I think, again, what that speaks to is if you're using Kickstarter or Indiegogo or any other platforms to communicate your updates, I mean how exciting is it, look there's an update from your project, wow, I mean really, wow. Whereas the blog was a story and it was an evolving story and it was, like, today's episode is this. And I tried very much to end on a cliffhanger, where I could. You can't a lot of the time, and sometimes I would break big events into three or four blogs and I'd literally end with 'and then... to be continued'.

STEPHEN: I got phone calls from people who knew I knew you, and at least two people, including my current business partner, who I wasn't in business with then, called me up and said, 'Could you tell him to stop doing this, tell me what the next thing is.' That was a motivation beyond just me calling you. People were calling me and I had nothing to do with it, I was more a witness than anything else.

CHRIS: I think ultimately every human being is a storyteller. Some people don't know it but they are and some people get fobbed off into writing an update; here's my bullet points on my Excel spreadsheet or my PowerPoint presentation of facts. And human beings are not interested in facts, they're interested in journeys and stories, so you should package what you're doing in a story without falling for your own bullshit or being self-piteous.

STEPHEN: Do you think filmmakers suffer from that much?

CHRIS: My big gripe with many filmmakers is entitlement. It's like, even if you want me to read your update, earn the time, because I'm going to give you my time now. For me, that's my most precious resource, so earn that time. Whether it's 10 seconds or 60 seconds or 5 minutes, or 5 minutes and a warm fuzzy glow and click with some money, you have to earn all of those things. You're not entitled to any of them.

And the best way to do it is by engaging with me on a human level, not bullshitting me, inspiring me, telling me your journey in a way that causes me to take action in my own life. And I think that's why many people came to me after *Gone Fishing*.

I have a very specific story to share about somebody who didn't contribute who openly came to the premier and said, 'I didn't think you'd make it but I've seen the film now and I'm a little bit ashamed to admit I didn't give you £50, because I do think you'll win the Oscar now, I think it's so extraordinary. But also you don't know this, but I suffered from cancer and the NHS were so good to me, and my cancer is so rare that there's really not enough resources and the people who looked after me were amazing, but I can see they were stretched. So I want to do something about that and you've inspired me to take action. Something else you don't know about is, I've always wanted to swim the English Channel, so I'm now committing to swimming the English Channel in the next two years.'

She did it and we made a video blog about the whole journey. She swam 52 miles in 18.5 hours and raised £25,000 for charity. The impact on her personally was so significant that she, pretty much over the next three years, rose through the ranks in a major pharmaceutical firm, one of the top three, and she's now the head of HR in that company. And that all happened after she swam the Channel and people said, that's an extraordinary human being that can do that.

She raised her own goal, she raised her own aspiration levels. We didn't cause her to get into a cold lake every single Sunday morning for four hours, but we catalysed her into 'I want to and I'm going to commit'. And that's because we became, in that moment, her peer group and an outstanding peer group will raise the standards.

So, by doing that through your work and creating an environment, a blog, a Facebook page, however you do it, that is very aspirational, that is aiming high, failing routinely but fessing up to failure in a way that says, 'I've learnt from this, I'm now going to attempt something from a different direction,' and maybe failing again, and not trying to look good all the time, because nobody is interested in that. We can smell the bullshit for miles, but just fessing up and saying, 'This is failing but we're never going to stop.'

That's so aspirational. It will change the people who are contributing to you. It will change their lives also and that's when they'll become addicted to the relationship because everybody is getting something life-changing out of it. And we've gone from 'I want to make a short little film' to 'We're going to change lives', and suddenly that feels like something that, actually, I really want to be involved in. That's the game we should be playing.

STEPHEN: Okay, my very last question: what happened with the Oscars?

CHRIS: So, we got to number six of five nominations. I know this because I had an informant inside the Academy, because she… actually, I've just given away too much there. This person started following the blog and was like, 'This is really cool, you're sharing all this data which is inspiring people.' So this person started dripping me tiny little… it was almost like Deep Throat. This didn't come from me so I can tell you this.

So I found out that we were six of five. Independently I found out from someone else because they were at a screening of the ten and they sent me the programme, and there it was in the programme. And of course I'd got an email from them and a request for four prints, or three prints of the film, which would be DCPs now.

It was painful to know that we were number six of five, but you know, I often talk about this in seminars: life is a journey, life is a story, and the essence of a story is to bring meaning to meaninglessness or meaning to chaos or meaning to failure, because in life, if we're playing the game, we're more likely to fail than to succeed. It's only in films that we succeed very often. And if you're succeeding at everything in your life, you're playing a very small game.

So films are an opportunity to bring order to that chaos. I played the game big and I didn't get the result I wanted, but I got a different result, which was equally outstanding and extraordinary and has enriched my life beyond any imagination that I had at the time. I just thought I was making a short film; I didn't realise there was a completely separate effect of the film, which was people.

People would see the film and come to me afterwards – these are generally people over 40, not always, but generally, who probably lost somebody recently, because the film deals with bereavement in a very happy, upbeat sort of way. And there would be tears coming down their face, saying, 'I have to have a copy of the DVD to give to my sister because it shifted everything. She will so get it; it will really impact on her.'

And that's when I realised that there's a kind of missing spoke in the filmmaking experience because we're so used to creating stuff and putting it out there. As human beings we're evolved creatures who, 20,000 years ago, would be sitting around a campfire telling a story and we'd be present at the telling, so we'd get that immediate feedback, that immediate relationship with the audience.

But with filmmakers, with musicians, you record a CD, you make a film and you put it out there, and you don't get that feedback in the same way. And that's why big concerts for musicians are so important because they have to have that relationship, and for filmmakers that's why festivals have endured, because you can get that relationship.

Because actually, logically on a business perspective, festivals are stupid because you spend a lot of time and money presenting your film to people, you don't get paid for it, you won't get a cut of the box office; in fact, all you get out of it is the warm, fuzzy feeling of having your film screened to people who get it and who like you and who want to like you.

STEPHEN: *Validation, isn't it?*

CHRIS: The validation, significance, the possibility of an award you might get, which in and of itself is fundamentally useless. Unless it's an Oscar or a BAFTA or the Sundance, or Cane, there's probably seven awards in the world that will actually make any difference. I know this because I had a key meeting with a top producer and I walked in very pumped up and saying, 'Hello, I'm so awesome, here are the 47 festivals *Gone Fishing* has won,' and he took one look at the list and threw it in the bin, and he said, 'I don't care about that, tell me how you're going to make me money.' And I was like, okay, I'm now playing a different game. I was playing that game at that level; I'm now in a different world playing a different game.

STEPHEN: *That got you into the room. It's like a key is useful to get in but at that point you don't need it any more.*

CHRIS: Exactly, exactly.

STEPHEN: I guess one of the things I've definitely picked up from this chat is the journey worked because you interacted with people, and, if anything, that is what filmmaking is about and what filmmakers are about. It's all an extension of putting yourself out there to communicate as a human being and interact with people.

CHRIS: Because that's when they'll give more, you'll get more, and it might inspire other things for them later on. Really, fundamentally, the best asset is yourself, but you have to tell the truth. It can be a version of the truth, a story version, but it can't be the bullshit version. It can't be the good-looking version or the one where I'm not going to admit to failure or defeat; people want the truth. And that's an edited version of the truth, it's a shorter version of the truth, and it's probably, I would suggest, an inspiring, 'I'm keeping going' version of the truth. But they don't want the bullshit version.

MARK TAPIO KINES
WRITER & DIRECTOR

STEPHEN: So I guess I'll start with, what's your background and what were you up to before you started the film?

MARK: Well, I went to film school at CalArts, north of Los Angeles, to study. Technically I was in the experimental animation department. They have two departments in animation. One is for character animation and most of those guys wound up at Pixar. Actually, most of those guys wound up starting Pixar. And then we had the experimental animation division, which was sort of freeform. To give you some examples, my classmates, the year I graduated, one wound up creating Sponge Bob Square Pants and one wound up directing *Kung Fu Panda*, and actually he's directing a version of *The Little Prince*, which I think is coming out next year.

But I wound up making live-action films at CalArts, that's what I wanted to do. In 1996 I finally had an idea for a feature film that I felt was filmable. So I wrote it; it became *Foreign Correspondents*. I was sort of introduced to a producer in 1997 who read the script. I was going to make this film for about $30,000 or $40,000 dollars in 1997. That was the plan. I had that amount of money in the bank, saved up from my job, and I was going to shoot it on 16mm, with friends, do it non-union, shoot it in people's apartments, that seemed very doable.

And as I said, I was hooked up with this producer in 1997 and she read the script and said, 'We can make this for more money than that.' She had just finished a short film, which she had raised some, I don't know, $50,000 for, so she said these two guys who funded this film, they really want to make a feature and basically she put all her eggs in one basket.

Long story short: she eventually raised our budget to $500,000 and got nothing from these guys and actually got nothing from anybody. I think she wound up raising herself, as the producer, as the owner of the film, she actually bought my script for one dollar so we could have a contract for it. So she raised $10,000 of the half million dollars she needed. We had already spent $90,000, which was the $40,000 I had put in personally and the $50,000 I had raised from two friends, $40,000 from one and $10,000 from another.

We were supposed to start shooting one Sunday in July or August 1997, and that Friday I said, 'Well, we spent $90,000, we've raised nothing else, this is supposed to be a $500,000 film.' And I asked my producer, how many days can we shoot before we run out of money? She said, one. So that weekend I spent with emergency calls to family. I was trying not to get family involved; I don't have a rich family but we're all capable of saving up a little bit of money. So I said I needed some money just to try and get this film in the can.

Literally, my mother and my father and my grandmother wired me money as loans – well, they were meant to be loans, they were never paid back. Friends sent me some money for loans which were paid back, and eventually we were able to get the film in the can over the 18-day shoot. And remember, this is a 35mm production, we were shooting on location in California, we had an SAG cast and we had a large crew of some 40 people. It was a full-on production.

After we wrapped, everybody was owed money. All the cast, the crew, the vendors, everybody was owed money. We literally just had enough money to buy film and food to feed people with. That was it, everything else was gone. So I didn't know quite what to do. My producer was obviously useless at this point, she wasn't going to do anything, she was not able to do anything. She's a very good manager but not a good fundraiser.

Because I was a web designer I knew there was one way in which I could promote the film for no money and that was, I could just set up my computer at my job and make a website for the film, since that was one thing I knew how to do. Just to get the word out. We had some actors who had a following, like Wil Wheaton and Melanie Lynskey.

I said, 'Well, there's fans out there, maybe we can find them and see if we can get the rest of this film funded.' So I raised enough money on my own to pay off the one person I really needed to pay off first, which was the stills photographer so I could get pictures. That was very necessary, and of course back then it wasn't even digital, they were slides. So yeah, I paid her off the couple of hundred bucks she was owed and I got the stills and I set up the website.

And I just kind of left it at that. I said, 'Well let's see if anybody finds this.' I set up the website at the end of '97, in November. And I was literally just asking for money, just kind of begging. I said here's the film, this is what it will look like; it's not that different, actually, from how people do crowdfunding now. Except that back then no one would have even considered the possibility of just giving money to a production. The concept was that it had to be an investment.

So I wasn't saying, send me $30 or $50 and I'll get you something. It was like, if you come in at $500 or more we'll write a contract for you and you can own part of this film. So around that time, a little bit later, I had the idea to offer, for people who didn't want to give that much money, stills from the film at $15 for four. Just four 4x6 glossy photos that I would snail mail. So people would literally send in paper cheques for $15 and I would send the photos. As far as I know, those are the very first perks that were ever devised.

Basically the site did nothing until it was featured on this thing that, back in '98, was still a big deal, called Cool Site of the Day. I don't know if you remember it, but that could really make or break a site back then. Which just goes to show you how small the internet was during those years. So yeah, I got Cool Site of the Day and I was lucky enough to hit it on a Friday so it was actually a Cool Site of the entire weekend, and that attracted attention.

It got me some guy who was a fan of Wil Wheaton, who put in $25,000 as an investment, and that really kicked everything off. And then, throughout the rest of 1998, it just came in, in small instalments. A thousand dollars here, five thousand dollars there; some guy eventually put in $75,000, I think. And then by the end of 1998 we were able to finish the film and premiered it in February 1999. So that's the basic story right there.

STEPHEN: *How did the film world react to the story of how you funded it? Because you would have thought with all the beauty of hindsight, everyone would have gone, 'Wow, I'm going to do that tomorrow.'*

MARK: It wasn't huge but I did get some notoriety from the press. Remember this was 1999, before the dot.com crash. So in 1999 the buzz was 'How do you make money on the internet?', and everybody was going to be a millionaire, and so I was seen as this entrepreneur who was spearheading a new way to make movies on the internet.

But then the dot.com crash happened and I think that scuttled the concept that you could raise money for anything on the internet. I think it became very trendy for a year or two to say the internet is over and let's think of pets.com, or whatever it was back then. Everything seemed like a joke, all these people who were trying to sell worthless goods online. And so I think that kind of quieted the concept of crowdfunding. We didn't even call it crowdfunding at the beginning, it was just me trying to raise money.

Honestly, Stephen, I didn't even think about it, and then a few years ago I was looking up the origins of crowdfunding and it said the first time it happened was in 2004, this woman in Britain and these two guys in France, and I said, 'No, no, no, I did this before they did.' Only difference was we didn't have an apparatus – it wasn't something you could just click on and use your credit card.

STEPHEN: Did you consider doing it again for your next film?

MARK: No, because, well, you know, it took a year and a half to make *Foreign Correspondents* and we had such a terrible time with money during that process. I got so angry at my producer and there was a lot of negativity. It's inevitable when you owe a lot of people money.

And I wasn't even the one liable. Legally, the producer owned the film, she owned the liability, it was her responsibility to pay everybody but she was physically unable to. I basically took on the burden of doing that myself and I didn't want to do that again – I felt I'd let a lot of people down because *Foreign Correspondents* didn't make any money.

So my second film was sort of like, okay, let me just self-fund this and see how it goes. And that was a different experience and then, yeah, I don't know, a third feature has never come around so I turned my attention to short films, which I could make for next to nothing.

You could see it as an isolated incident, the *Foreign Correspondents* thing. It happened six years before the next film attempted to do something like that. It was really kind of in a vacuum almost.

STEPHEN: What do you think of crowdfunding today? How does it compare to the journey you went on?

MARK: Well it's interesting to see what's sort of similar and what's changed. I think the downside is, right now, I personally don't know, in terms of films, how well it's going to continue to do. I think it does really well with documentaries because a documentary just oozes non-profit. People want to get involved because they care passionately about the subject and they're happy to throw their money away to see the film get made.

Whereas I think for people making features and fiction short films, there's always a sense of, well, the filmmaker is hoping to become rich and famous and it's a sort of hard thing to get behind unless the filmmaker is not looking to make much money and is essentially what I call 'friend funding'. That's where it's going to be people you know giving you money. I think this is a reality a lot of people don't want to talk about with film crowdfunding: unless you have a celebrity, or unless you have a documentary you can market to a passionate core audience, or unless you have a large YouTube following, where you're cranking out these short films and you have millions of views and thousands of followers, friend funding is what you'll have to do.

I think a lot of people have been burned at this point because a lot of filmmakers have not made their movies. I've given to several campaigns and the films never got made, simply put. And so, just as a backer, I would be very reluctant to help out someone like that. As a filmmaker it gives me extra responsibility to make the film. I did an Indiegogo campaign this year for a short film which we've just finished, and because I raised enough money we're screening it for backers on Sunday.

It's nice to see it can work but I feel the concept that a lot of people have of 'you should give me money to support indie film' is flawed. People will say that, they'll say that on Twitter: 'Hey, we're trying to raise money, support indie film.' As if indie film is a charity. But I think, at this point, so many people realise that indie film can be quite bad, and that it's not automatically good, that filmmakers who are independent aren't automatically saints or saviours or even special people. I don't know.

I would probably continue to try to use it if I had a good enough idea and I felt it was doable to raise a few thousand dollars. I don't think I would try to raise $100,000 through crowdfunding unless I felt it was something that could truly go viral. And I think the only way it can go viral at this point is if you have an insanely large following or if you have a celebrity involved who has an insanely large following.

STEPHEN: *It is interesting because it seems to me to be going the same route that Hollywood goes, where the big ones get bigger and the small ones get smaller. It all comes down to marketing and having a big name who is willing to get out there for you. It's like the gentrification thing where one area becomes cool, so other people come in and hike up the prices and kick out the original people.*

But my personal opinion is that crowdfunding is going the same sort of way, whereby it starts off with people going, oh look, this is our small little film. But as it professionalises, professionalising being the equivalent of gentrification, you end up in a place where you can't compete like you used to. And maybe it's natural, maybe it's part of the marketplace where there's so many more projects out there, so of course it's harder and of course over time things get more professional.

I was looking at some of the old campaign videos from very early Kickstarter projects and they're awful, they're terrible, they're badly made, they're just shoddy, and also the attitude is almost like, well, maybe this will work but give me your money, you won't get anything, and they're for the funded ones. But now you look at them and they're so slick and they're so well made, and maybe they should be, but it's a different world from what it was 2008/2009, and even more so from the world you were funding your film in.

MARK: I feel very ambivalent about the whole thing because people have gotten smarter. They know they're not just going to give $20 to some guy who wants to make a film, just because he says, 'I'm a nice guy and my film is going to be good.' A friend of mine who ran a successful, I think a $300,000, $400,000, campaign for a video game reminded me that people help with video games because they'll then get the game, and the thing with video games is that you spend hundreds of hours playing it. It's fun.

Whereas people don't really own movies unless it's a very big, special movie to them. So to be able to say, hey, if you give me $25 or $50, some people will even say $75 or $100, and you get a DVD of the film, that's not worth much to people because they know they're not really going to watch that film, possibly ever. And even if they did, it might just be once or, if they really liked it, twice.

But it's always been, I've noticed, an issue of perception between professionals and amateurs, in that if you don't have some kind of shepherd championing your project, and by this I mean it did well at Sundance, or you've got a celebrity involved or something like that, people are going to approach it as, oh, this is amateur hour. It can't possibly be good.

People want to have fun. I think one of the reasons I did all right with this last crowdfunding campaign I did for the short film was because the stuff I offered was fun. The movie is called *20 Matches* and it actually involves a girl lighting matches, and I said, if you give $20 I'll make a little matchbox figure out of clay, of anything you want, and I'll put it into a little matchbox I'll make myself and I'll send it to you.

This has turned out to be a massive amount of work for me, but everybody is getting an insanely good deal because, for $20, I'm working for, like, four hours making these perfect little figures that are only two inches tall. But it's fun for me to do, it's a creative project, so I have no complaints. But I think it was one of those things where people thought, 'Well, I don't really want to see the film but that looks cool, that looks like something I would want to have.'

I think people tend to forget that filmmakers tend to be egotistical, they tend to think everybody is going to love this film, I'm going to make the best film ever, and you'll be a fool not to get in on the ground floor because it's going to win Oscars, and it's going to get 20 trillion YouTube views and you're going to feel bad for not helping. But everybody else is like, okay, well, there you go. The truth is somewhere in the middle. Because it's a creative act, there is no objective truth. Some people will love it and some people will hate it, no matter what it is.

STEPHEN: But what matters is how many people will pay for it.

MARK: Yeah, so bragging rights are fun, and that's why it helps to have something people can feel passionately about, because it says something about themselves, like, 'Oh, I funded this documentary, and even if I don't see it, I like to be able to say I helped get this important movie made, or that I helped out this project a famous person was working on, and as a result I got a funny little video of this famous person saying my name and I can post it to Facebook and tell everyone.' You know, that stuff is cool.

STEPHEN: I wonder if people are curating their Kickstarter biography profiles the same way they do when they buy lots of books to fill up a shelf to say, 'Look at the kind of person I am, look at the books I own. I don't write them but I own them.' Like, you know, 'I chipped in $5 for that documentary, I'm changing the world.'

MARK: Kickstarter does have that little colour wheel where it's almost like Trivial Pursuit: you can fund projects in all the different sectors and each sector is represented by a different colour, so, on your profile page, you can get your little wheel filled in.

STEPHEN: You know, I did that, and the reason is because I was doing this research into crowdfunding and I wanted to compare it to a few other creative things I thought were similar, other creative arts. But one of them that had absolutely no relevance was food; like, it's got nothing to do with what I'm doing so there's no point. Because I was giving $5 here and there, just to different campaigns, just to see the experience.

But then the colour wheel wasn't quite complete and I'm a neat freak, I wanted it to be neat, and so I chipped in $5 or $10 or whatever it was, and the person emailed me when I sent it and they said, where shall we send this chocolate thing? And I was like, no, I don't want it. What do you mean you don't want it? I was too embarrassed to tell them why but it was just for that piece of the pie, that's all I wanted, I didn't want the physical pie.

MARK: It's funny because I've helped out a number of campaigns, one or two because I thought they were cool, mostly because they were with friends or with friends of friends and I just wanted to help out because what's a dollar here or there? I don't usually give $20 or $50, I'll give $10 or $15; it's not a big deal and you're kind of a heel if you don't. Especially once you've been through it and you realise how much of a struggle it can be to get even a couple of dollars from someone who calls themself your friend. It means a lot to someone to know you're willing to take a chance on them.

I do it more, and I don't think I've ever asked for a perk, mainly because, as I was saying, they don't seem that much fun and they're not really worth having in the house. You don't want to accumulate more stuff, a bunch of DVDs you'll never watch, a T-shirt you'll never wear, or this and that. And, unfortunately, I think a lot of filmmakers struggle to find interesting things to offer, besides the movie or a T-shirt, and I wonder how many of them are doing nowadays. Like I said, it's mostly friend funding. If you can't offer someone bragging rights for getting involved in your film, most people don't really want the stuff.

STEPHEN: I think you're absolutely right. The conclusion I've come to is the film is a McGuffin and you are a McGuffin in the sense of how much it actually means to you. Basically you're in a reality TV show and, if it's interesting, people will watch it. What I mean is, they'll give you money so they get to watch the journey through updates or whatever.

But if you're not as interesting as the next thing on the next internet page, which could be a cat on a skateboard, then they're off. So if you manage to be entertaining, whatever entertaining means, you know, coming up with a product no one has thought of or being fun or whatever the thing is, like in your case the little things you're making, that's great, that's interesting. It doesn't need to be interesting for hours on end, it needs to be interesting for a short period of time, but that's enough to earn the money. Crowdfunding is dancing for the money and that's fine; loads of people do it but know that's what it is and rehearse.

MARK: That is true and I'll say one other thing: I don't know if it's relevant but for this last short film that I did, that I did the Indiegogo campaign for, at least three strangers came in at relatively high levels. I mean I wasn't asking for a lot of money so you didn't have to give $5,000 or anything like that, but one fellow in Switzerland came in for $500, a fellow in Malaysia or Indonesia came in at $100 and a fellow in Canada came in at $100. They were essentially collecting executive producer credits to add to their IMDb page.

That was one thing I offered. I said, if you do this I'll give you an executive producer credit and I'll put you on the IMDb page. And that meant a lot to them because it was their goal to present themselves to the world as these film producers. So again, everybody gets involved for different reasons, but it was interesting. I had so few strangers give money to this and three of them came in at high dollar marks because that's what they wanted.

STEPHEN: Well, yeah, if they're buying the credit and you're going to deliver the credit, then actually it's not that they care or not, it's irrelevant; it doesn't change it because nobody is going to judge the film before they judge their credit. They're not going to go, 'You're an executive producer, but let me watch the film before.' All they're going to see is, ah, 20 credits on IMDb as an executive producer going back for ten years – well, you must be somebody. There's an honesty to that, I guess.

It's funny, you reminded me actually, when I gave money I gave myself $100 and said I'm going to give it to loads of different films and see what it's like. Just live it and also support some different people. I got probably three or four of them coming back to me, sending me personal messages after I donated around $5, next to nothing, saying, 'Oh my God, I don't even know you, this is amazing, you're not even from my town, how did you even find out about it?'

And I thought, that's just sweet. But thinking back, based on what you said, you're right, it was a shock that shouldn't really be there if they're genuinely crowdfunding it, because this should be like, yeah, this is very nice of you but this is what we set out for and this is what we're doing. But for some of those I might be the only person they don't know.

MARK: And on the flip side of that I ran an unsuccessful campaign for a feature last year, and I made sure I thanked everybody who came in, whether they were a friend or a stranger. And there was a fellow in Sweden who I wrote to, I said thank you, and he said, wow, I've given to so many campaigns and almost nobody running these campaigns ever says thank you. They never send a personal message.

And I was shocked to hear that, that someone could be so entitled that they wouldn't even take a few seconds to say thank you. I mean it's one thing if you're getting thousands of contributions and you can't say a personal thank you to every person that comes in at $1, but for most people they're only getting a few hundred over the course of a month and you can certainly handle a few hundred over the course of a month.

I was surprised, and I think also that's kind of why a lot of people might feel burned about helping filmmakers, because, unfortunately, a lot of filmmakers – it's always been the case, it was the case in the nineties and it's the case now – are kind of full of themselves. You have to be a little delusional to think your film is worth making. But the dark side of that is some people can be a little arrogant. They can't even humble themselves to say 'thank you for giving me money, you stranger you'. They're kind of the first people you should thank: 'Wow, you gave me money, thank you so much.'

COLIN BROWN
EDITORIAL DIRECTOR AT SLATED

Since this interview took place, Colin Brown has left Slated, *so his views may no longer reflect current thinking at the company.*

Colin is now an Adjunct Professor at New York University Stern School of Business and also a Managing Partner at MAD Solutions, an innovative Arab film and TV studio that markets, distributes and finances independent storytellers.

STEPHEN: My first question is just to ask you to sum up Slated, and the history of Slated, and where it sits in that whole crowdfunding environment.

COLIN: It's been functioning for four years; it was launched in January 2012. When it was formed, I think the question it tried to answer – and it's gone through several evolutions in answering that – was 'Why isn't investing in film as simple as investing in the stock market?'

So that was the guiding inspiration behind it. Now, there are lots of reasons as to why it's not as easy as investing in the stock market, but in order to answer that, a two-sided marketplace was created. We concentrated on getting in as many film industry creators as possible, with the emphasis on producers and film companies on one side, and buy-in from the industry and investment community on the other.

STEPHEN: So how does it compare to other crowdfunding? What's the same, or different, about Slated compared to Kickstarter?

COLIN: Well, that's why I mentioned the stock market, because when you invest in a stock, you don't do so thinking you're just donating your money, or that you're doing it for patronage. So, I guess the analogy is that Kickstarter and Indiegogo in their original forms were more like charity and non-profit. You're putting money into a cause you believe in; you support it, you're passionate for it. The reward you get from it is seeing it being made and getting a certain amount of pride out of that. With the stock market you invest because you think the stock has growth prospects.

I have to say, one of the issues I sometimes face when I write stuff for Slated on the platform is the word 'crowdfunding'. There are at least two different understandings of that phrase. You mention the word crowdfunding, most people automatically think only of the donation platforms, right? Because they've done very well and a lot of films have turned to them.

The average raise for a film – successful films, that is – isn't very high. I doubt it's in five figures; it could be, but it's probably about eight or nine thousand dollars, or something like that, it's not a vast amount of money. So the value to a production isn't financial so much as validation. It shows there's a market demand and that there's real value, especially now, because getting distribution is actually, arguably, the bigger problem than getting a film financed. At least you can show a crowd-level of buy-in, which is an illustration of potential market demand.

There's often a gap between what the market will offer you and how much you need to make the film. If you have a risky film (i.e. one that's not very commercial), you won't get many people wanting to invest or many pre-sales. So, once you've tapped out the soft money (e.g. tax breaks you get for filming in certain areas), you can still be left with a funding shortfall.

This is where Slated comes in. We felt there were several market inefficiencies. One was that the pool of investors you could turn to, given the size of the film marketplace and the interest level in film, was surprisingly small, and there are any number of reasons for that. It's seen as a very difficult place to invest.

Frankly, I think a lot of investors don't treat film as a proper investment anyway. It's unduly complicated, it's tarnished with all sorts of bad reputations, and it's high profile, so the bad examples get amplified in the press, making it a very offputting place even compared with other circled, or alternative, investments. So people have fewer problems, it seems, investing in fine arts, or wine, or any other alternative investments you can think of, than they do film.

So what we've learnt along the way, by the way, is that, as much as we can try and encourage investors and grow the investment pool, which is what the original aim was for film, we also had to educate the marketplace about investing in film as a concept, and to simplify it and make it more transparent, and that's taken us a long time.

On the way there, and I think this is a crucial evolution that Slated has gone through, we enjoyed some successes in terms of raising large amounts of money for films and projects, some unusual ones. There was a film in an Indian language, it wasn't Hindi even, it was a lesser-known language for Indian cinema, a drama. An Indian investor based in New York put money in on Slated, whereas the filmmaker was based in Paris, and the production was shot in India. Called *Sunrise*, it did very well on the festival circuit, and it was completely unexpected for us – we didn't expect that Slated would be a vehicle for money going into an Indian film, via another Indian, through New York, and so that was a bit of a light-bulb moment where we saw that the need for such a matchmaking platform is on a global level.

There were other films, documentaries and star-driven films, that raised money on Slated. But after a while, I think – and this is my own personal way of looking at it, not necessarily the official view, but at its most extreme – what we realised was that Slated was getting films made that probably would have got made anyway, but faster.

So the community is very strong, it's a top-tier producing and filmmaking community, a lot of the films listed on Slated have some sort of elevation in the marketplace, but the question was, 'Are we adding anything to the overall picture?'. It's very useful to accelerate but are we widening the kinds of films that should get made, or would get made, or can get made, that audiences want to pay for, and are we widening the kinds of people that are willing, and would happily invest in film, but just had no real reason or easy entry point to do so?

The big addition to all this was that we started a very elaborate scoring system. Everything on Slated, whether it's a company, whether it's a person, or whether it's a project, gets scored. You can imagine the challenge it was for me to explain that to an industry that has resisted the application of data because they think of it as the enemy of creativity.

It's similar to the venture capital industry, certainly when it comes to tech start-ups: they're literally having to take a punt on ideas that haven't been proven yet; that's the whole point of venture capital, right? So how does it do that, and why does there seem to be more money pouring into tech start-ups at an early stage than into film?

There are two things they do. One is that, instead of measuring the idea, they give up on the idea, because the point is, there are no yardsticks. They measure the team and they also measure where the ideas are coming from, where did they receive them, what were the channels, who's validating them. They look at the combination of the people involved with it, their own track record, how they've dealt with failure in the past, as well as successes, how they've built on that, blah, blah,

blah. That's one level. Then the other thing is that they invest small amounts of money into a very, very, very large range of investments.

So, both of those things are appealing to Slated because we'd say, 'Okay, we wouldn't need to have a way of assessing ideas, rather the team behind them, and we will also want to see people invest across a much, much wider slate of productions, rather than one, or two, or even five.' Again, the stock market analogy.

STEPHEN: So, if a filmmaker is looking for the right platform to raise money in the crowdfunding world, what kind of projects would be best on Slated?

COLIN: Let me pick up a thread I left hanging before which answers this. We'd said, 'How are we going to get films made that under the normal circumstances, would never get made,' right?

A good example of that might be *Whiplash*. I use *Whiplash* as an example because *Whiplash*, on paper, should never have got made. And I don't say that judgementally, or artistically, because I think it's a fantastic film, but literally, it would never have got made under normal circumstances.

How do I know this? It was a 3.3-million-dollar production and the filmmaker who wrote it, Damien, had never made a feature-length film. So that was one mark against his person because first-time filmmakers are really difficult to back. Also, there were no known stars in the film.

A producing company did the estimates and I think the estimate was, you'll be lucky if you get half a million out of the film marketplace. But they loved the thing so much they decided to take a punt and fully finance it themselves because they believed in what they saw, the filmmaker, and they chose the cast that was right for the film.

So how do you get more films like *Whiplash* made? Well, you've actually then got to score the projects themselves based on their own creative elements. The first question people ask of any project isn't, 'Okay, who's directing it?' but actually, 'Who's in it?'. The answer to that only demands a very short list of actors. And, of course, there's the catch-22: you'd love to have those actors (although, often, they're actors who wouldn't be appropriate for the film) but you can't afford them, right? Because that's why you're raising money. So the actors say, 'Do you have the money?'. You say 'No'. The investors say 'Do you have the actors?'. And you say 'No'. And so you're stuck in this limbo-land. So how do you break through that?

Well, you've actually got to create a new currency, sort of a pre-sales currency: you've actually got to score the projects based on their inherent strengths.

Slated worked with a client that asked for data on 10,000 films. They broke those films down to a granular level that was unbelievable. They didn't want to just know who was in it, what the genre was, what the two-line description was; they wanted it scene by scene, and various things like, night, day, moods, all these sorts of things. Using this data a system was created for valuing screenplays, and this is where it gets interesting.

To test it, we then took out all the identifying data on projects that had happened in the last year, the name of the film, for instance, and who was in it, and ran it through the system. We asked it to come up with projections on, in this case, the North American box office, and at varying budget levels. The results were plus/minus 11%, okay?

We then compared that to what the tracking services did, the Hollywood Tracking Services that the studios use for the same films. Their results were plus/minus 23%, okay? And then here's the kicker: their results are based on tracking surveys done two days before the release, so all the available knowledge about that project has already been factored in, including how many theatres it's going to be released in, what the marketing campaign is, early buzz, all that sort of thing. We were doing it at script stage, so, like, two years before that, and we're getting it twice as accurately, or rather, the data was doing that twice as accurately.

STEPHEN: *Do you struggle with a communication problem there? Because I remember hearing that from you guys a while back, and it wasn't that I didn't believe it, it was just that it was so different; it's a whole different revolutionary thing and I'm sure it's verifiable, I'm not doubting it, but it's hard to swallow because it's hard to relate it to anything else in the experience of film, and related within film.*

COLIN: Well, I share the same scepticism, but I've had to change my own view on data. By the way, I sell this because *Whiplash* was one of the films that was crunched through this, and one of the things it said was, this project based on its own thing would generate in the global marketplace $20 million. It's actually done much better than that, but $20 million was way better and more accurate than the half million they were told when they financed it, a 3.3-million-dollar production.

In other words, if you'd been told that, you liked the short film, and that this at a base level was going to do $20 million worldwide, you would invest in that film. Certainly at the 3.3-million-dollar budget.

STEPHEN: *Whose algorithm is this; where does this currently sit, who is currently using it?*

COLIN: So, the algorithm sits in an entity called Slated Analytics, which has just got its... and this is a bit of legalese... it's a registered investment adviser, which is an SCC-approved vehicle for all the scoring and everything like that. Because it now falls in the court of investment advice, it has to be housed in a registered investment.

STEPHEN: It sounds like quite a significant investment to be developing all that, that data gathering and breaking things down, and then also, using people who know numbers, who know what they're doing.

COLIN: You're right, it's actually a rather substantial investment, but it's being paid for – or hopefully paid for – by selling the investment services, and then in time, also, now we're in the syndicating business, we do actually take fees for raising money.

STEPHEN: Do you know the old adage about who made the most money during the Californian gold rush?

COLIN: I think the answer is, it was all the people selling the pants.

STEPHEN: Yes, it was Levi Strauss.

COLIN: And to some degree, the brothels.

STEPHEN: Actually, yes, that's a nice addition to the story, yes. It was the guys building the tents and the pans, you're right.

COLIN: And I've used that myself, because what a great analogy. Yes, Slated is in the business of selling the pans. We're not prospecting for gold, we're selling the tools by which you can prospect for the gold, and yes, you're absolutely right. But we also have to be very careful. I don't know how much due diligence was done back then; I'm suspecting that when you gave someone their pan and shovel, you weren't then saying, 'By the way, you're never going to find any gold.'

STEPHEN: Yes, but you might have the same effect saying it to filmmakers today. Well, one of the last things I just need to grab is the type of projects Slated wants, and is best for, because obviously you're not going to do the £5,000 short film, or the micro-budget feature film.

COLIN: Well, if you'd asked me that a year ago, I would have said, you're right. But now we're in this new paradigm; all the barriers have come down so anyone can join Slated, but you get scored, and therefore, there's no need to have any artificial barriers.

I think that's important anyway because budgets, while they're an indicator, are not the only indicator of market appeal and, in fact, some of the biggest outliers and some of the greatest returns on investment are obviously with ultra-low-budget films. They can literally come out of nowhere, so why should we try and second-guess that? So it's now very much an open market.

Films from micro all the way up to… it doesn't really matter at the top end either… are on the platform and investors can invest in whatever. If we keep the financial analogy going, to me, the goal here is to allow for different types. You can construct a portfolio of investments across industries.

So you can say, 'Okay, I'm going to do blue-chip stocks, I'm going to put 20% in that, those are my boring ones but I'm going to get dividends; I'm going to put some in foreign markets, emerging markets, some high risk but higher returns potentially; I'm then going to do some complete start-ups, probably going to lose my money but if they hit… so I'll put 5% in there.' Well, that kind of thinking could apply to film as well.

The blue-chip stocks are presumably the films with guaranteed global distribution, let's call them studio films. And then, all the way down, like your penny stocks and your opportunistic ones, would be the low-budget ones, and you could have foreign-language films as well, because, actually, the ROI picture and the PNA spend, it's very dramatically different so there's a bucket to put your investments in, and you could create portfolios based around that, as opposed to portfolios based around genre and slates, which I think is a mistake. We'll have one horror film, one romantic comedy, one this, one that – that's not a very sophisticated way to invest in films.

STEPHEN: I agree completely. There are some projects that are going to live best on these ones where you're basically asking for the kindness of strangers, but then there's Slated, and Slated is something different because you need a business plan, you need to have a commercial edge to your film; although that doesn't mean it couldn't be, in theory, a similar film, you've just got to take a completely different approach to prepare the package and whatnot. So what do they need for it to survive on Slated?

COLIN: We score screenplays across 11 different criteria. One of the criteria is literally originality, so if it hasn't been seen before, that would actually score really well, because actually… if you've ever read any of the things I've written, there's one of the things I keep repeating to the point of boredom, I think, and that is, I keep saying, if there's one element – and I say this as a former film critic as much as anything else – if you were going to distil the one element behind successful films, the element to me is surprise, right?

And that's the other paradox: the financing industry, particularly the banks who then have to come in and back the paper you've got, don't like surprises. I mean, it couldn't be any more of an anathema to the banking industry, the word surprise; literally, they do everything and they don't want a surprise there.

STEPHEN: If you don't have any surprise, what you need is a massive marketing budget, because it occurs to me that a lot of the studio affairs, especially the stuff

*we think is drivel that does well – so sequels, knock-offs, spin-offs, Transformers 8 –
that is the opposite of surprise because you're buying a ticket for the same comfort,
in the same way that when you go to McDonald's, you get exactly the same thing,
but when you go to a new restaurant with a good chef who's been well trained, you
get surprised.*

COLIN: It's not blind acceptance. I'm not a big *Avengers*-type person, a big fan;
however, I read the reviews of these things and I go to some of them and it's
interesting. Within the context of big franchise movies and sequels, people do
demand originality. The response to the different Harry Potter films, for instance,
varies, depending, I think, to some degree on the director, who brings their own
sensibility to it and comes up with something fresh. Maybe that's a better word
than surprise.

Look at *Star Wars*. Chances are, I think the excitement of the new one is the
feeling that at least J.J. Abrams is going to bring back some of the freshness and
come up with a new take on what would have been a law of diminishing returns.

Paranormal Activity, by the way, probably has just suffered that. I think it was
probably done by rote, the new one, and it's done really badly. Marketing will only
get you so far, and I think actually, right now, it's because of social media and
the way people communicate; it's very difficult to actually market your way out of
problems, and it's a global issue too because the news comes out so fast.

The way you combat it is, it's not so much the surprise, it's not so much by
marketing, although that helps; it's through having great producers. If you talk to
the bond companies, the way they look at things is: there's two types of risk in a
production, right? There's execution risk and there's performance risk. They know
performance risk is the thing that's very difficult to do anything about, and to some
degree, that is the crapshoot; you don't know how well, two years down the line,
an audience is going to respond, because there might be something like it or the
mood has changed, we may have gone into a war, who knows – any number of
factors which are beyond your control could come into play there.

On the other hand, execution risk, which is actually the biggest problem, is
completely manageable. Will this film actually get made, do the people know what
they're doing, and will it get made in the way the people backing it understood it
to be when they put their money in it? And that is very much about the team, what
have they done, do they know what they're doing, can they handle the budget?
Having a Hollywood producer on a micro-budget film is as much a disaster as the
other way around, because their expectations about where you spend money and
how you save it, and use the money, are completely wrong in the context of the
production, so it's about having the right team.

Which gets us back to the VC world. It's about the team and the entire thing, starting with the writer, because it's the script, but then you have to think about all the other elements that surround that original idea.

STEPHEN: You're absolutely right. One of the worst First ADs I ever hired, professional First ADs, was a First AD on one of the Bond films and was doing me a favour, and did an atrocious job because he just didn't know how – and it's not his fault, he's obviously incredibly talented – he just didn't know how to do it when you didn't have the army of people, and I'm sure most generals in the field couldn't go out and kill someone hand-to-hand tomorrow, but they could lead people to do the job well, and I think it's the same thing. So you're absolutely right, it's appropriateness more than just a single scale.

So, last question I guess is, whether it's one tip or a load of little tips, what would you say to filmmakers who are putting their film on Slated, to help improve their chances of securing investment?

COLIN: Well, all right, that's a really good question. All right. Several things I would say. Slated works best, I think, if people treat it as if they were their own sales agent at a film market, right? And I say this because it's surprising how little they do that, so they'll put a project on there and then say, 'Well, nothing happened,' and we'll say, 'Well, what did you do? You have to be the agent of your own success here.' And of course they didn't do anything, so there are lots of things you can do.

There are some things people have learnt from the Kickstarter world, which is that you arrive on the platform with as much momentum as you can possibly muster, so you pre-bake your success to some degree. You have to get to a certain percentage of your raise within, I don't know, a week. If you get 10% of your money within the first few days, your probability of getting your 100% – which is important on Kickstarter, not so much Indiegogo – is so much higher.

In the context of Slated, when you arrive, you want to have got the thing as well supported as you possibly can so that people are following it in this context, tracking it, so you get the sense that people are all clicking on something in a day, you're alerting people to something that has got momentum behind it.

Now that there are analytic services, you can use them to bolster your score. While a project that's got a high score financially, or a high score creatively, will do better on the site because it will be directed towards investors, if it actually – quite literally in one case – hits a certain threshold score, it will then be put in front of investors. It's a self-syndication model. There's the other syndication model, which is for certain projects; they are then presented on a much more bespoke basis to investors whose criteria they match.

So there's that, and then I'd say, everyone should do their homework in the way they should anyway in the marketplace, which is, okay, what have you got realistically? Have a very realistic idea of who's going to be watching it, what its main appeals are likely to be, what its likely market size will be, where are they and do you have a route to market?

And then start reaching out, almost ahead of time, to those people and say, 'Look, I'm going to be putting a project on Slated, I think it's the kind of thing you'd be interested in,' either as distributor, or as a sales agent, or even as a packaging agent in some cases, so that you're presenting it in the best possible light, as opposed to just leaving it up there.

One thing I haven't seen done, but I don't know why it isn't, is trying to present things in different ways. Why not try different taglines, different descriptions, different images to go with it, just to see, because you might find that – especially with a documentary – there's some elements of it that appeal to somebody's sense of philanthropy, let's say, or a cause? Let's say it has music by so-and-so, and an investor is obsessed with that musician, they just didn't know that was part of the project, so they say, 'Okay, I'll do that,' just to be associated with it.

So people should come as fully prepared as possible, but then also, I think, just experiment a little bit and tweak the message to maximise the possibilities.

STEPHEN: That makes sense. We do so much of that stuff in our everyday work; we use pre-rolls on YouTube, and we do AB testing, we do focus grouping, not because... not to supersede the human part of the whole thing but because it helps to have something tested, and also, it allows us to be more scalable, because if you only make projects that appeal to you, so you can use your own intuition, you're limiting yourself, whereas if you say, 'I'm going to build a system where I don't need to know deep down in my waters which is going to work, I can go out there, test it and repeat it, and then do it again here, and do it there.'

COLIN: Absolutely. The only danger I'd say in all of this, and I say this outside of Slated, just as an observation, having worked heavily now with a data-driven company and seen the advantage of data, I've also seen the dangers of data, which is a complete reliance on it, because data is only as good as the questions asked of it. So you have to be darn sure about the questions you're asking, that they're going to give you the results that are useful, and I think people have forgotten that the best data and the best analytics in the world are our own brains, right?

Take social media. The great stuff about social media is also its peril, because social media data is so easy to get to, and so it becomes the only thing used in decision-making. And yet, we know that not everyone is on social media and people's response to social media can be misleading, because the most important people don't always have time to respond to something on social media, right?

STEPHEN: I think Twitter especially. I'm on Twitter, but pretty much because I have to be, and I use it to put out my blogs. But one thing I have noticed when I've tried to engage in it is, it's such an echo-chamber of the 1%, a different 1%, but you do get sucked into thinking it's important. But I think it's like living in one part of town and never leaving; you start thinking it's the centre of the universe because it is, to you. It is in your universe, it's just not the universe, and I think, just as travel broadens the mind, I think online travel broadens the mind.

COLIN: It's a tool, that's all it is, and it's a fantastic tool. We've never had any of these things and it's going to help the creative industries immeasurably to solve those things I mentioned in the beginning, which is, it's just not broad enough. It's a cottage industry that actually does think of itself as industry – it should be a bona fide business in the way that any venture capital or risk business is a bona fide business.

Treat it seriously, measure it seriously, but also, it's dealing with human emotions and so on, so therefore I think human emotions will be coming into the assessment of all that data that's coming at you. So it's both, and I think both have to be done in tandem, absolutely, and crowdfunding seems to be the place where the two come together, I think, really nicely.

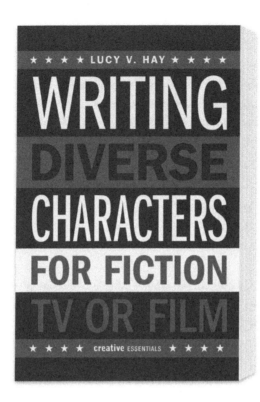

WRITING DIVERSE CHARACTERS
FOR FICTION TV OR FILM

We're living in a time of unprecedented diversity in produced media content, with more characters appearing who are Black, Asian and Minority Ethnic (BAME), Lesbian, Gay, Bisexual and Transgender (LGBT), disabled, or from other religions or classes. What's more, these characters are increasingly appearing in genre pieces, accessible to the mainstream, instead of being hidden away in so-called 'worthier' pieces, as in the past.

Writing Diverse Characters discusses issues of race, disability, sexuality and transgender people with specific reference to characterisation – not only in movies and TV, but also novel writing.

kamerabooks.co.uk/diversecharacters